新世纪英语专业听力教程

(1)

Accumulate Your Listening Experience

李岩　陈则航　编著

北京大学出版社
北　京

图书在版编目(CIP)数据

新世纪英语专业听力教程(1)/李岩、陈则航编著.—北京：北京大学出版社，2001.8

ISBN 978-7-301-04923-5

Ⅰ.英… Ⅱ.李… Ⅲ.英语－听说教学－高等学校－教材 Ⅳ.H319.9

中国版本图书馆CIP数据核字(2001)第25805号

书　　名：新世纪英语专业听力教程(1)
著作责任者：李　岩　陈则航　编著
责 任 编 辑：汪晓丹
标 准 书 号：ISBN 978-7-301-04923-5/H·0605
出 版 发 行：北京大学出版社
地　　址：北京市海淀区成府路205号　100871
网　　址：http://www.pup.cn
电 子 信 箱：xdw777@pup.pku.edu.cn
电　　话：邮购部62752015　发行部62750672　编辑部62767347
出版部62754962
印　刷　者：北京飞达印刷有限责任公司
经　销　者：新华书店
850毫米×1168毫米　大32开本　11.375印张　280千字
2001年8月第1版　2008年1月第4次印刷
定　　价：17.00元

内容提要

《英语专业听力教程系列》以培养“积极主动会听之人”为教学目的，实践一种全新的教学理念，并且已经在北京师范大学等院校的英语听力教学中适用多年。全套听力素材均选自国外最新教科书和广播电视节目，语言语音语调多样化，融知识性、趣味性于一体。

本书为该系列教程中的第一册，供英语专业一年级一学年使用。旨在指导学生从理性与感性两方面系统学习不同类型英语口语的特点，积累听英语的经验，学会听。并配有磁带。

前　言

《新世纪英语专业听力教程》是为了在英语专业听力教学中实现培养“积极主动会听之人”这一课程目标而编写的教材，其教学理念和素材已在北京师范大学外语系英语听力教学中运用数年，得到了学生的认可和欢迎，对他们顺利通过四、八级专业英语的听力测试，提高听的能力起到了较好的作用。

在研究和分析学生的听力水平，听力训练中出现的问题的同时，我们特别关注和比较了“听”的技能在母语和外语中表现出的极大反差。在相关的听力教学理论的指导下，确定了听力教学的关键是如何采取行之有效的措施，帮助学生尽快成功地将母语中运用自如的听力技能转换到听英语的活动中来。这套教材就是以此为教学中心，系统安排和指导学生在相关的训练中，学会以听的手段获取知识和信息，交流情感和经验；在听的实践中，了解和熟悉以口语形式出现的英语，摸索出适合自己的听力策略和技巧，养成良好的听的习惯，掌握听的方法，提高听的效率，成为“积极主动会听之人”。

《新世纪英语专业听力教程》全套教材共四册，每学年一册。第一册 Accumulate Your Listening Experience，第二册 Challenge Your Listening Ability，第三册 Note-taking in Academic Listening，第四册 Critical Thinking in Advanced Listening。第一册和第二册是听力课的基础训练，第三册和第四册是高级听力训练。第一册教材力图指导学生系统地从理性和感性两方面学习不同类型英语口语的特点，积累听英语的经验。第二册教材的重点是让学生意识到听力策略和技巧的必要性、重要性和可行性，引导他们在实际生活中灵活并熟练地运用这些策略和技巧。第一册和第二册的基础训练结束后，学生应该具有独立学习和提高听英语口语的能力，即了解和熟悉英语口语的基本类型及其特点，掌握一定的听力策略和技巧，懂得自己该听什么，怎样听。第三册教材则是在此基础上，引导学生通过提高记笔记的能力，了解和掌握听学术报告和讲座的方法和技巧，实现以听为手段，在自己感兴趣的领域进行学习和研究的目的。第四册集中指导学生听有相当难度的访谈节目。

由于训练目的各异，每册书的侧重点和训练方法也各有不同；但全套书的教学宗旨是统一的。

听是一个检验听者的语言、思维等多方面综合能力的行为，听者不是在被动地接受信号，而是在积极地进行预测、辨别、判断、推理等多种活动。因此，提高学生的积极性，促进学生的主动性是教学成败的关键。

听不是目的，只是实现学习研究、进行交流和交际等目标的手段。因此，帮助学生了解英语口语，了解自己的问题及其原因，摸索出适合自己的有效的听的方法，养成良好的听的习惯，是教学的中心。

要帮助学生改变对英语口语的恐惧感和听英语时的焦虑心情，变“怎么这么快”，“怎么这样说”为“原来就应该是这样”的心态，积极主动地调整自己，以适应不同速度、不同声音的英语口语，积累经验，提高应变能力。

教学中要不断修正学生对听力效果的期待值，强调听的目的是获取信息、进行交流，而不是要听清楚每一个单词。听的内容中总会有生词和听不清的词，如何处理和应对这种情况则是对每一个听者听的能力的挑战。

这套教材旨在通过选用的材料，实践一种新的听力教学理念。在整套教材的计划、实施、实验、总结和调整过程中，我们始终得到了北京师范大学外语系和英语教研室领导和有关老师们的热情鼓励和大力支持，得益于外语系资料室和语言实验室的老师们经常的支持和帮助，得力于历届参与上述听力教学活动的学生们的配合和支持。在此，我们向他们致以真诚的谢意。

说　明

“Accumulate Your Listening Experience” 是《新世纪英语专业听力教程》系列教材的第一册。

听的能力是每一个健全人与生俱来的，听的技能是每一个正常人在生活、学习和工作中的实践中逐渐发展起来的。然而大多数英语学习者，特别是经过了小学、中学阶段英语学习的学生们，虽然掌握了基本的英语语法知识，具有一定的阅读能力，但在听英语时总感到力不从心，原有的听力技能受到了极大的制约和限制。“Accumulate Your Listening Experience”就是要帮助学习者通过积累听英语的经验，为尽快地、有效地摆脱这种制约创造条件。

本册书力图根据听在生活中的实际功用去指导学习者积累听英语的经验。同时，本册书还特别安排了介绍英语口语和书面语的区别以及英语口语特点的听力练习，以便学习者从理性的角度积累听英语口语的经验。

本册教材共有二十个单元，每个单元分为四部分：

Section 1　Listen Accurately

Section 2　Listen to Share

Section 3　Listen to Acquire

Section 4　Listen Efficiently

第一部分为天气预报、机场航班报告、学校课程咨询等各种场合中对听的准确率要求很高的内容。第二部分为反映时代变化、学校及各种社会生活的情景对话和小故事，第三部分是有关英美概况、英语学习的报告和讲话。这三部分内容丰富，具有趣味性和知识性，可以帮助学习者提高听的兴趣，体验听英语的快乐，激发渴望交流的欲望；各部分所设计的特定练习，既可引导学习者跨越语言障碍，达到进行交流，获取信息，学习知识的目的，又能增进对英语语言和相关文化的了解和理解，为继续学习打一个好的基础。第四部分为介绍、讲解和演示英语口语特点的内容。所选的听力材料有助于学习者在听的过程中，发现、认识、了解和熟悉英语口语的特点，改变按照对于英语书面语的了解，带着能够听清楚每一个字词的期待去听英语的习惯，提高对英语语音信号的辨别能力，学会听的方法，保证听的效果。

各部分互相配合，从感性和理性两方面指导学习者积累听英语的经验。各单元第四部分的内容既可随各单元其他部分一起练习，也可自成体系，单独进行训练。使用者可以根据需求灵活掌握。

按照"培养积极、主动会听之人"的教学目标，本教材的练习特别强调学生的积极参与，重视学生间的互动活动，希望学生养成良好的听力习惯，成功地积累听英语口语的经验。

为了帮助学生更好地克服在听英语时遇到的困难，我们在教学中已经尝试着实践了第四部分的内容，得到了学生的认可和欢迎。

它是根据成年人学习语言的特点，按照语言学中对于语音的声音形态及其变化的最简要的描述，以及它们与第二语言学习者听力活动的关系而安排的。本册书的第四部分以讨论听英语时所感到的困惑开始，从描述和介绍英语口语与书面语的区别入手，引导学习者在听英语的实践中，了解和熟悉英语口语的特点，掌握英语口语的一般规律，学会如何听英语。为了配合各单元中第四部分的学习要点，使学生同时从理性和感性两方面加深对英语口语的认识和体会，大部分的听力内容分别选自讲授英语语音、语调或英语口语的专门教材。

由于各单元的学习要点也常常是学习者在听力实践中感到最棘手的问题，例如(linking)连读等，因此在做相关练习时会感觉很吃力。遇到此种情况时，不必沮丧，也不要慌。因为英语学习者往往是以对英语书面语的了解来对待英语口语，出现这种现象很正常也很自然。这个时候要注意：

1．借助答案和文字材料完成练习。

2．对难点反复听，也可进行适当的模仿练习，以加深印象。

英语语音的变化、英语口语的特点、连读、省略与合并，辨音等练习的设置是为了引起学习者对于英语口语中这类现象的注意，通过反复的练习，逐渐熟悉和习惯地道的英语口语，走出对英语口语期待的误区。节奏，基本句子重音及其变化，语音语调的作用及其变化，意群等练习的设置是为了帮助学习者了解英语口语的一般规律，以减少听的障碍，更好地有效地将母语中运用自如的听力策略和技巧转换到听英语的活动中来。

在教材的编写过程中，参阅和借鉴了下列书籍和教材，选用了其中的听力素材。

1．Michael Rost.（1990）*Listening in Language Learning*，Longman

2．Mary Underwood.（1990）*Teaching Listening*，Longman

3．Judy B. Gilbert.（1991）*Clear Speech*，Cambridge University Press

4．Pamela Rogerson，Judy B. Gilbert.（1993）*Speaking Clearly*，Cambridge University Press

5．Stacy A. Hagen.（1988）*Sound Advice*，Prentice Hall Regents，Inc.

6．K. James，R.R. Jordan，A. J. Matthews.（1986）*Listening Comprehension and Note-taking Course*，Collins

7．John McDowell，Christopher Hart.（1988）*Listening Plus*，Edward Arnold

8．Barbara Bradford.（1988）*Intonation in Context*，Cambridge

University Press
9. BBC English, 1992, *Britain Now*
10. Kathy Gude. *Advanced Listening and Speaking*, Oxford University Press
11. Adrian Doff, Carolyn Becket. (1991) *Listening 2* Cambridge University Press
12. Adrian Doff, Christopher Jones. (1995) *Listening 4* Cambridge University Press
13. Adrian Doff, Carolyn Becket. (1991) *Listening 1* Cambridge University Press
14. Sandra Schecter. (1984) *Listening Tasks* Cambridge University Press
15. Deborah Gordon, Andrew Harper, Jack C. Richards. (1996) *Tactics for Listening* Oxford University Press
16. Marie Hutchison Eichler. (1991) *Against All Odds* Heinle & Heinle Publishers
17. John & Liz Soars. (1987) *Headway* Oxfort University Press
18. Jan Bell, Roger Gower. (1992) *Matters* Longman
19. Keith Harding & Paul Henderson. (1994) *High Season* Oxford University Press
20. Andrew Littlejohn, Diana Hicks. (1996) *Cambridge English* Cambridge University Press

在此,谨向有关作者和出版单位致以衷心感谢。

编　者

2001 年 7 月

Content

Text

Unit 1

【Section 1】 Listen Accurately

Numbers: numeral system

Task Listen carefully. Write the numbers as they are read.

(1)______ (2)______ (3)______ (4)______ (5)______
(6)______ (7)______ (8)______ (9)______ (10)______
(11)______ (12)______ (13)______ (14)______ (15)______
(16)______ (17)______ (18)______ (19)______ (20)______
(21)______ (22)______ (23)______ (24)______ (25)______
(26)______ (27)______ (28)______ (29)______ (30)______
(31)______ (32)______ (33)______ (34)______ (35)______
(36)______ (37)______ (38)______ (39)______ (40)______

【Section 2】 Listen to Share

A story: A difficult woman

Task 1 Before you listen to the story, try to discuss with your partner: What kind of woman can be called "a difficult woman"?

Task 2 Answer the following questions after you hear the story.

(1) What kind of woman is their grandmother?

(2) How often did they visit their grandmother and how long did they stay with her?

(3) How far did their grandmother live from their town?

(4) What happened one Friday when the mother went shopping?

(5) What did the mother do when she got the bad news?

(6) What actually happened?

【Section 3】 Listen to Acquire

The geography of the United States (1)

Task 1 Listening for specific information. Fill in the map with the names of the oceans and the nations you hear in the recording.

(1)_____ (2)_____ (3)_____ (4)_____

1
2
3
4
UNITED STATES
Seattle
WA
OR
CA
San Francisco
Los Angeles
San Diego
NV
ID
MT
WY
UT
AZ
NM
CO
Denver
ND
SD
NE
KS
OK
TX
Dallas
San Antonio
Houston
Minneapolis
MN
IA
MO
AR
LA
WI
IL
Chicago
St. Louis
Memphis
MS
MI
Detroit
IN
KY
TN
AL
Atlanta
GA
New Orleans
OH
WV
VA
NC
SC
FL
Miami
PA
Philadelphia
NY
Boston
New York
ME
VT
NH
MA
RI
CT
NJ
DE
MD
WASHINGTON, D.C.
CUBA
HAITI
JAMAICA
Honolulu
HI
AK
Microsoft Map

Task 2 Fill in the missing information.

(1) The United States is a large country, covering ________ square miles.

(2) The two major mountain ranges are ________ and ________.

(3) The three large rivers are ________, ________, and ________.

(Note: For the mountains and rivers, please study the map in *Unit 2*.)

【Section 4】 Listen Efficiently

Listening and understanding

Part 1 Pre-listening Activities

1. Fill in the chart from your experience.

The year as an English learner	The year as a listener to English	The year you've been taught to listen to English	The purpose for you to listen to English

2. Exchange your ideas with your partner after you have finished the exercises below.

(1) Choose the words that can best describe your emotions involved in listening to English.

Words and expressions

enjoyed, frustrated, excited, bored, amused, struggled, exhausted, stimulated

(2) Summarize your experience of listening to English in 3 or 5 sentences, you may choose one of the following as the beginning of your summery.

① The most important thing in listening is ________.

② The most difficult thing in listening is ________.

③ The most interesting thing in listening is ________.

Part 2　Listening Task

1. Are you interested in knowing the opinions of an export on listening? Here is a lecture on listening. The following questions can help you follow the lecturer, so read them before your listening, and listen for the answers in the lecture.

   (1) How many problems in listening has the lecturer mentioned?

   (2) What is the order by which he has arranged them?

   (3) Why is it hard to recognize the words in spoken form?

   (4) What kinds of activities involved in listening according to the lecturer?

2. Listen again for the details mentioned in the following statements and check your comprehension of the lecture by telling true or false of the statements.

(1) It is as easy to identify words in speech as in print.

(2) The problem of identifying weak forms and unstressed syllables only occurs in speech.

(3) It is not difficult to remember what has been said because it can usually be heard more than once.

(4) When students understand and remember all the words they usually follow the argument.

(5) A more colloquial style of speech is less easy to follow than a more formal one.

Part 3 Post-listening Activities

Discuss the topics below in pairs.

(1) Name any other problems you've been bothered with, though not being covered in the lecture.

(2) Have you ever had a listening course in Chinese? Why do we need a listening course in English?

(3) What do you expect to do in a listening class?

Unit 2

【Section 1】 Listen Accurately

Numbers: hundreds, thousands

Task 1 Listen carefully. Write the numbers as they are read.

Examples: one hundred twenty-three—123

eight hundred ninety-four thousand five hundred sixty-seven—894, 567

(1)______ (2)______ (3)______ (4)______ (5)______

(6)______ (7)______ (8)______ (9)______ (10)______

(11)______ (12)______ (13)______ (14)______ (15)______

(16)______ (17)______ (18)______ (19)______ (20)______

(21)______ (22)______ (23)______ (24)______ (25)______

(26)______ (27)______ (28)______ (29)______ (30)______

(31)______ (32)______ (33)______ (34)______ (35)______

(36)______ (37)______ (38)______ (39)______ (40)______

Task 2 Listen and fill in the blanks with the numbers you hear.

Cookies are a big business in the US. One shop in Boston sells

①______ warm cookies every day, mostly chocolate chip. On the West Coast, a ②______-year-old American, Wally Amos, has made his fortune from chocolate chip cookies.

When Amos was ③______ years old, he went to live with his Aunt Delia, who made cookies for him, from a recipe created in ④______. Amos joined the Air Force in ⑤______, and his aunt sent him cookies so he wouldn't be homesick. For Amos, as for most Americans, cookies represent love and home.

After the Air Force, Amos worked for other people for ⑥______ years. In ⑦______, he decided he could make more money if he had his own business. He talked some friends into investing $ ⑧______ in a cookie business. He worked ⑨______ hours a day, baking cookies and thinking of clever ways to promote them. For instance, he traded $ ⑩______ worth of cookies for advertising time on a local radio station. In ⑪______, he began selling cookies in ⑫______ department stores on the East Coast. That year the cookie corporation took in $ ⑬______. By ⑭______ the company made $ ⑮______. Amos now has ⑯______ employees, and they produce more than ⑰______ pounds of cookies a day.

【Section 2】 Listen to Share

A story: meeting famous people

Task 1 Before you listen to the tape, discuss with your partner if you meet a famous person somewhere what you would do.

Task 2 Listen to the story and answer the following questions.

(1) When and how did "I" meet a famous person?

(2) What did "I" do a weekend?

(3) Why couldn't "I" stay at Savoy hotel? And where did I stay?

(4) When did the taxi come and how did "I" feel at that time?

(5) Why did that man want the taxi take him first and what did he promise?

(6) What was in the newspaper the next day?

【Section 3】 Listen to Acquire

The geography of the United States (2)

Task 1 Listen for specific information. Circle the following names on the map according to the introduction you hear.

Coast Valleys	North East	Great Plains
Mountains & Deserts	South East	Central Basin
Alaska	Hawaii	

Pacific Ocean
HIBISCUS
Kauai
Niihau
Oahu
HONOLULU
Molokai
PEARL HARBOR
PINEAPPLE PLANTATIONS
Lanai
Maui
Kahoolawe
WAIKIKI BEACH
Hawaii
MAUNA LOA
HAWAII

Arctic Ocean
BARROW
ESKIMOS
NOME
Arctic Circle
OIL FIELDS
FAIRBANKS
MT. McKINLEY
HIGHEST N. AMERICAN PEAK
Bering Sea
ANCHORAGE
SALMON
JUNEAU
Pacific Ocean
ALASKA

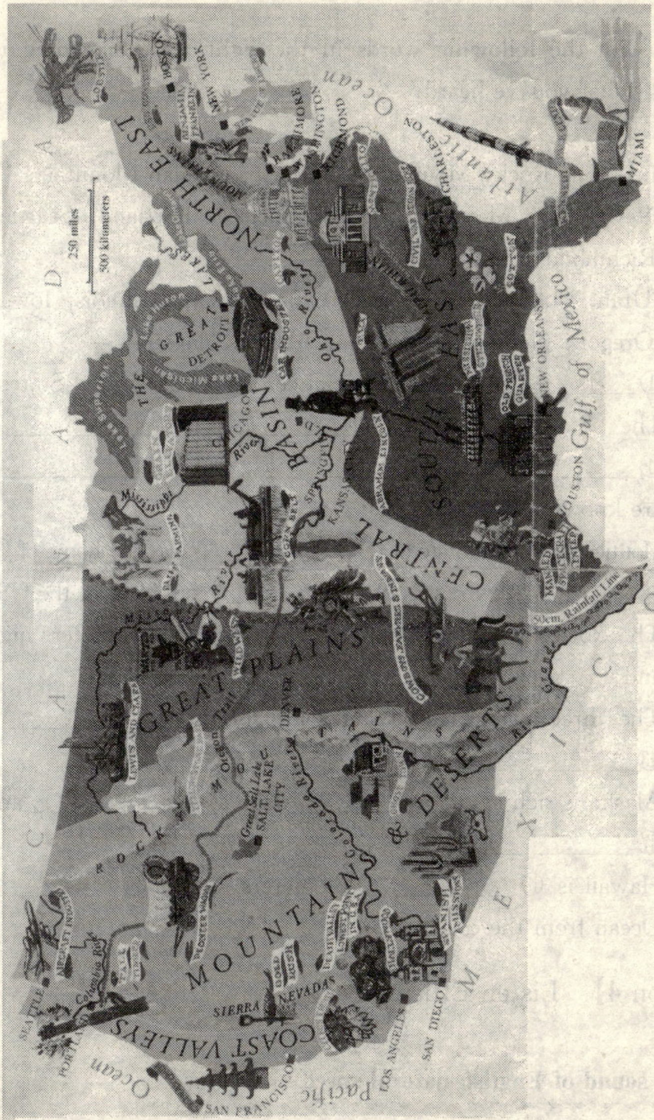
250 miles
500 kilometers
CANADA
NORTH EAST
THE GREAT LAKES
CENTRAL BASIN
SOUTH EAST
GREAT PLAINS
ROCKY MOUNTAINS
MOUNTAIN & DESERTS
COAST VALLEYS
Atlantic Ocean
Gulf of Mexico
Pacific Ocean
MEXICO
BOSTON
NEW YORK
BALTIMORE
WASHINGTON
RICHMOND
CHARLESTON
MIAMI
NEW ORLEANS
HOUSTON
DETROIT
CHICAGO
DENVER
SALT LAKE CITY
SEATTLE
PORTLAND
SAN FRANCISCO
LOS ANGELES
SAN DIEGO
SIERRA NEVADAS

Task 2 Put the following words in the right place according to what you've heard.

Mountains: The Rocky Mountains, The Appalachian Mountains

Cities: New York, Monticello, San Francisco, Portland, Seattle, Richmond

States: Utah, Colorado, California, Ohia, Indiana, Illinois, Iowa, Oregon, Nebraska, Virginia, Alaska, Hawaii

(1) ①__________ is the financial center of the United States.

(2) The States of ② __________, ③ __________, ④__________, ⑤ __________, and ⑥ __________ are known as the Corn Belt.

(3) Monticello, in the State of ⑦__________, was the home of ⑧ __________, who was ⑨__________ president of the US.

(4) The Rocky Mountains are over ⑩__________ meters high and ⑪__________ kilometers wide.

(5) The three Pacific coast states are ⑫ __________, ⑬__________ and ⑭__________.

(6) Alaska is rich in ⑮__________, such as ⑯__________ and ⑰__________.

(7) Hawaii is ⑱ __________ kilometers out in ⑲ __________ Ocean from the coast of ⑳__________.

【Section 4】 Listen Efficiently

The sound of English natural speed

Part 1 Pre-listening Activities

1. Read the transcript of the lecture we've listened in *Unit 1* on page ×.
2. Listen to the lecture again with an eye on the transcript, and mark out any words you missed in your listening practice in Lesson 1.
3. Talk with your partner about the missing parts, with a focus on the ones you both have missed, and note them down on the sheet below.

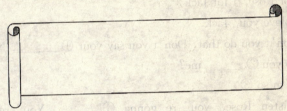

Part 2 Listening Task

1. Read the two sentences below and listen to them with your attention to the bolded parts.

Art is **man**'s att**empt** to imp**rove** on **na**ture.

Are **these man**'s **attempts** to im**prove** on **na**ture?

(Note: Have you noticed the difference between the parts bolded and the parts without being bolded in your listening?)

2. Listen to more sentences and write them down one by one on the lines below.

(1) ______________________________

(2) ____________________

(3) ____________________

(4) ____________________

(5) ____________________

(6) ____________________

(7) ____________________

(8) ____________________

3. Listen to the famous dialogue in the film *Titanic* and fill in the blanks for the lovers.

(R for Rose, J for Jack)

R: I love you, Jack.

J: Don't you do that. Don't you say your ①______ . Not yet, do you ②______ me?

R: I'm so ③______ .

J: Listen Rose, you're gonna ④______. You're gonna ⑤______and you're gonna make lots of babies, and you're gonna ⑥______them grow. You're gonna die and old, an old lady warm in her bed. Not ⑦______. Not ⑧______, not like this, do you understand me?

R: I can't feel ⑨______.

J: Winning that ticket, Rose, was ⑩______ that ever happened to me. It brought me to you. And I'm ⑪______ for that, Rose, I'm ⑫______. You must, you must do me this ⑬______. You must promise me that you'll ⑭______, that you won't ⑮______. No matter what happens, no mater how ⑯______, promise me now, Rose, and never ⑰______, promise.

R: I ⑱______.

J: Never ⑲______.

R: I'll ⑳______ Jack. I'll ㉑______.

Part 3 Post-listening Activities

Pair work:

With the help of the questions below, sum up the differences between written and spoken English from the practice in this lesson and your experiences of learning English.

1. Is the word easier to obtain by reading or listening?
2. Are there any advantages we have in reading taken away in listening? What are they?

Unit 3

【Section 1】 Listen Accurately

Names, addresses and telephone numbers

Task 1 Listen to the tape and write down the names and places.

(1) ____________________ (2) ____________________

(3) ____________________ (4) ____________________

(5) ____________________ (6) ____________________

(7) ____________________ (8) ____________________

(9) ____________________ (10) ____________________

Task 2 Listen to the tape and write down the telephone numbers.

(1)______________ (2)______________ (3)______________

(4)______________ (5)______________ (6)______________

Task 3 These addresses have mistakes in them. Listen to the tape, and write the address correctly.

(1)

John Michael

50 Brown Place

OXFORD

Tel 323-7690

(2)

Jo Hardman

The Washington Building

2563 Orchard Road

SINGAPORE

Tel 263 7453

【Section 2】 Listen to Share

Hotel check-in

Task Listen to a conversation between a receptionist and a guest checking in without a reservation. Put the information in the chart.

	Information	
Name of guest(s)		
Number of guests		
No. of nights		
Room type	□ Executive □ Twin □ Smoking	□ Standard □ Double-bedded □ Non-smoking
Address		
Method of payment		
Reserved	□ Yes	□ No

【Section 3】 Listen to Acquire

Schools in the United States

Philosophy of American Education

Education in the United States has been shaped by the American belief in a free, democratic society. In turn, education has helped to shape that society. The survival of a democracy depends upon the intelligent participation of all its citizen. Every American needs to be educated so that he can understand and take part in affairs of government, both local and national. He must also have educational opportunities to develop vocational skills. Education is the key that opens the doors to responsible citizenship and a productive life. American believe that every citizen has both the right and the obligation to become educated.

Task 1 Listen for specific information—Fill in the blanks.

(1) According to the article, there are ①______ kinds of schools in the United States. They are ② ______, ③ ______, ④______, and ⑤______.

(2) There are clubs in high schools such as ⑥______, ⑦______, or ⑧______.

(3) Some of the high school students' favorite sports are ⑨______, ⑩______, ⑪______, and ⑫______.

Task 2 Listen for comprehension—True or False?

(1) It takes six years for American kids to graduate from high school.

(2) College students spend more hours in class than high school students everyday.

(3) As long as they attend classes, college students can pass their examinations.

【Section 4】 Listen Efficiently

Some characteristics of spoken English

Part 1 Pre-listening Activities

1. Exchange your opinions on the differences between written and

spoken English with your partner and focus on your ideas on spoken form of English.

Written English	Spoken English

2. Discuss the following descriptions about spoken English and check the ones you agree on.

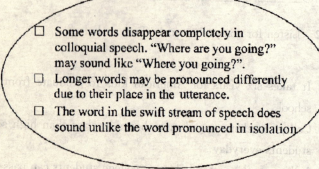

- ☐ **Some words disappear completely in colloquial speech. "Where are you going?" may sound like "Where you going?".**
- ☐ **Longer words may be pronounced differently due to their place in the utterance.**
- ☐ **The word in the swift stream of speech does sound unlike the word pronounced in isolation**

Part 2 Listening Task

1. Listen to the opinion on the question why it is hard to understand spoken English. Read the exercise to get the framework of the opinion and then listen and fill in the missing words.

Every ①______of every language is within every ②______. So, what happens with ③______? People learn their ④______ language and stop listening for the sounds they never hear; then they ⑤______ the ability to hear those sounds. Later, when you study a foreign language, you learn a lot of ⑥______ that take you still further away from the ⑦______ of that language—in this case, English. The trouble after you know a great deal of English is that you know a great deal ⑧______ English: You have a lot of preconceptions and, unfortunately, ⑨______ about the sound of English. What we are going to do here is to teach you to ⑩______ again.

2. Listen to the talk on the difference between written and spoken English. Read the exercise to get the framework of the opinion and then listen and fill in the missing words.

You may have notice that I talk ①______ and often ②______ my words together. Native speakers may often tell people who are learning English to "slow down" and to "speak clearly". This is meant with the best intentions, but it is exactly the ③______ of what a student really needs to do. If you speak fairly ④______ and with ⑤______ , you will be understood more ⑥______ .

By seeing and hearing ⑦______ , you'll learn to reconcile the differences between the ⑧______ of English (spelling) and the ⑨______ of English (pronunciation and the other aspects of accent).

Just like your own language, ⑩______ English has a very ⑪______ , ⑫______ sound. If you speak ⑬______ , you'll end up ⑭______ and ⑮______ .

Connect words to form ⑯______ . Instead of thinking of each word as a unit, think of ⑰______ , which make a sentence flow

⑱______ , like peanut butter—never really ending and never really starting, just ⑲______ .

3. Listen to the talk on accents.

Read the exercise to get the framework of the opinion and then listen and fill in the missing words.

Accent is a combination of three main components: ①______ (speech music), ②______ (word connections) and ③______ (the spoken sounds of vowels, consonants, and combinations). Part of the difference is that grammar and vocabulary are ④______ and ⑤______—the letter of the language. Accent is ⑥______ , ⑦______ and ⑧______ —the spirit of the language. You can use your accent to say ⑨______ and ⑩______ . Word stress conveys meaning through ⑪______ or ⑫______ , which can be much more important than the actual words that you use.

Part 3 Post-listening Activities

1. Summarise the characteristics of the sound of English conveyed in the excerpts of the talk you've heard.
2. A demonstration of the difference between written and spoken English is provided here to reinforce your ideas on the characteristics of spoken English.

(1) Listen to Alison and decide which of the following pictures corresponds to what she is saying?

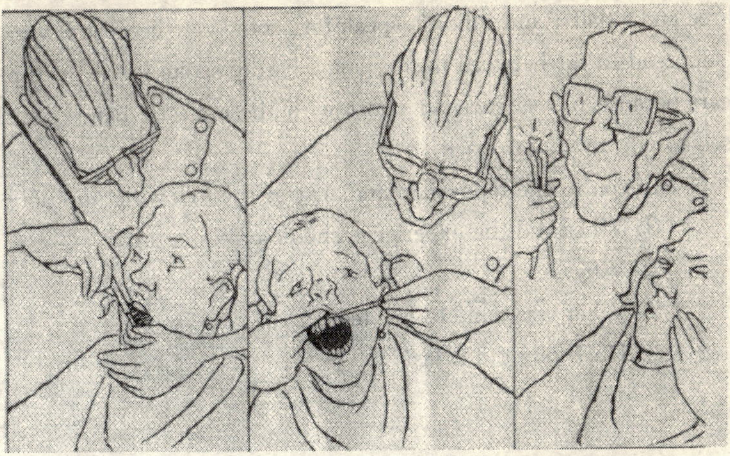

(2) Now read the transcript. Can you tell the difference between the written and the spoken form of her talk?

When I was about 13 they said, "you're going to have a brace", and I thought "Oh yeah, you know, a simple little band round my teeth", and they, they showed me this picture and I had to have it top and bottom, and every tooth was ringed round with metal and a metal tab put on the front, and then a wire linking all the teeth together. I don't think that they need to do that, because my teeth, stuck out like that, because I sucked that finger, and all I had was a metal band, one thin band across. But mine were sort of like a zig-zag along the bottom. And a real mess, weren't they? Ah, I see. And the eye teeth were, yeah, I had hoops on my eye teeth. Sort of, they're very good now, aren't they? Ninety degrees, ninety degrees round. Oh, I see. And then I had elastic bands linking my top teeth to the bottom teeth. Oh my God. Because my jaws were in the wrong order; and I had this on from thirteen... they said it was going to be on for a year and it was on for three and a half ; and I didn't speak for about . . . because I wasn't supposed to eat between meals, and I hardly spoke for about three years because it was such an effort with these elastic bands which used to pin my mouth back.

(3) Listen to the tape again and answer the following questions.

① When did the experience she describes occur?

② Why?

③ What was done to her teeth?

④ How long did it last?

Unit 4

【Section 1】 Listen Accurately

Times and dates

Task 1 Listen and write down the time you hear.

(1)________

(2)________

(3)________

(4)________

(5) ①________; ②________; ③________; ④________

(6) ①________; ②________; ③________; ④________

Task 2 Listen to the telephone messages and write down the time and date as well as the event.

	Dates and times	Events
(1)		
(2)		
(3)		
(4)		
(5)		
(6)		

【Section 2】 Listen to Share

A story from Vietnam

Task 1 Listen to the story and then put the sentences in the correct order.

A. The taxi driver turned round to ask the girl some questions, but she wasn't there.

B. He saw a young girl under a tree near the road.

C. On his way home it started to rain heavily.

D. An old woman came to the door.

E. The girl got into the taxi and the taxi driver drove her home.

F. She went back into the house and closed the door in the taxi driver's face.

Task 2 Answer the questions. Use short answers.

(1) Did the taxi driver finish work in the afternoon?

(2) Was he cold?

(3) Did it start to rain?

(4) Did he see a young man?

(5) Was the girl under a tree?

(6) Did he drive the young girl home?

(7) Did she give him some money?

(8) Did he talk to the girl's mother?

(9) Was the mother angry with the taxi driver?

(10) Was the girl alive?

(11) Did the taxi driver see the young girl again?

【Section 3】 Listen to Acquire

Higher education in the United States

Task 1 Listen for specific information—Fill in the blanks.

①________, ②________, and ③________ at universities give students higher education. Community colleges have two-year programs. Many students at community colleges study subjects such as ④________, ⑤________, and ⑥________. Both universities and colleges have four-year programs. Universities also have ⑦________ for students who want to do ⑧________ after they finish four-year programs.

Task 2 Listen for comprehension—True or False?

(1) There are graduate programs at community colleges.

(2) In order to get bachelor's degrees, students must finish their four-year programs at universities.

(3) Undergraduate students only study courses in their majors.

(4) For doctor's degrees, graduate students will study two years.

【Section 4】 Listen Efficiently

Linking (1)

Part 1 Pre-listening Activities

Read the following statements and tell true or false according to your own experience.

(1) Most university students learn a foreign language mainly through the printed page. This produces a tendency to separate words during speech just as they are separated in print, an unfortunate tendency for people learning English.

(3) As a result, linking is a major source of comprehension difficulty for non-native listeners.

Part 2 Listening Task

1. Listen to the recorded sentences and write the sentences down on the lines below. Then count the words in each sentence you've written and you've heard.

(1) ______________________________

(2) ______________________________

2. Listen to the conversations and fill in the blanks with the words you hear.

Conversation 1

A: We ①________ down First near James, heading toward the water. A car came ②________ the corner. I guess he didn't see ③________ may be he ④________ little drunk. Who knows! Anyway, he ⑤________ ⑥________, missing ⑦________ bikes by less ⑧________.

B: ⑨________?

A: No. ⑩________ what's more, he ⑪________looked back. Probably didn't ⑫________ he'd ⑬________stop sign.

B: ⑭________ he hurt ⑮________?

A: It wouldn't surprise ⑯________.

Conversation 2

A: ⑰________ that all about? I've never seen Bob so edgy. ⑱________ happen?

B: ⑲________ I know of . But I ⑳________ mention taking a day off and he about hit the roof. It's ㉑________ it's ㉒________ this week, either.

A: ㉓________him at all. Maybe he's under some pressure.

B: Possibly. I ㉔________ he wouldn't take it out ㉕________.

Part 3 Post-listening Activities

1. One element of natural speech is that words are not spoken separately but are linked together. There are two sorts of linking, read the examples and mark out the linking part.

   (1) Words ending in a vowel sound are linked to words beginning in a vowel sound.

   Example: you‿are I‿always we‿ought

   (2) Words ending in a consonant sound are linked to words beginning in a vowel sound.

   Example: sit‿up read‿it turn‿off is‿(h)e

2. Study the linking rules below.

Linking rules

   (1) Words ending in a consonant followed by words beginning in a vowel the final consonant links to the initial vowel, *eg* this

evening.

(2) Words ending in a vowel followed by words beginning in a vowel: the words are linked by inserting a sort of "w" or "y" sound, *eg* "w"sound-if the vowel at the end of the first word is rounded (*ie* has a rounded lip position).

"Y"sound-if the vowel at the end of the first word is spread (*ie* has a spread or stretched lip position), *eg* so(w) I'll, I (y)am.

(3) Words ending in "r" followed by words beginning with a vowel: the final "r"(although not pronounced in isolation in standard southern English) is linked to the next word, *eg* where is, are in.

Unit 5

【Section 1】 Listen Accurately

Money system

Task 1 In American currency

(a penny = 1cent   a nickel = 5 cents   a dime = 10 cents
a quarter = 25 cents   half dollar = 50 cents   a dollar = 100cents)

Now listen to the tape and try to write down the names of coins and the total cents.

Example:
5 dimes = 50 cents

NAME OF COINS	TOTAL CENTS
2 ________	
3 ________	
2 ________ and 2 ________	
3 ________ and 1 ________	
1 ________, 2 ________, and 1 ________	

Task 2 Listen to the cashiers and write down the money each person had to pay and the change they received.

	Total	Change
(1)		
(2)		
(3)		
(4)		
(5)		
(6)		

【Section 2】 Listen to Share

A story: Sunset Boulevard

Task 1 Listen to the story. In what order did these things happen?

A. Norma fell in love with Joe.

B. Joe put his car in Norma's garage.

C. Joe fell in love with a writer.

D. Joe met an old film star who was once famous.

E. Norma gave Joe a job.

F. Norma became famous again.

G. Norma killed Joe.

H. Joe tried to leave Norma.

Task 2 Find six mistakes in this summary. Then listen again and check your answers.

At the beginning of the film Joe is walking down a street in Los Angeles. He meets a young film star called Norma Desmond. She lives with her boyfriend in a big house in Sunset Boulevard. She gets a lot of fan letters from all over the world. Joe then moves into her house and writes a filmscript for her. He also falls in love with her. When he tries to leave her, she stops him and he kills her.

【Section 3】 Listen to Acquire

The Declaration of Independence

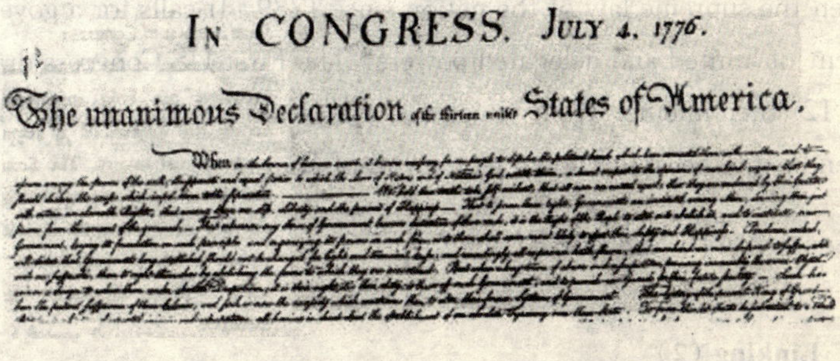
IN CONGRESS. JULY 4. 1776.

The unanimous Declaration of the thirteen united States of America,

Task 1 Listen for specific information—Fill in the blanks.

(1) The Declaration of Independence was largely written by ①________.

(2) The Declaration of Independence declared ②____________,

offered ③__________, and laid out ④____________.

(3) The Constitution of the United States was drafted in ⑤________ in ⑥________.

(4) Washington, DC is located between the States of ⑦________ and ⑧________.

Task 2 Listen for comprehension—True or False?

(1) The United States is a nation with a history more than 200 years.

(2) 15 original colonies broke away from Great Britain in 1776.

(3) The Constitution of the United States can be changed at times.

(Note: US Constitution—The Constitution of the United States has been the supreme law of the nation since 1789. It calls for a government of limited and delegated powers. The First US Congress drafted 12 amendments, from which the states ratified 10. Those 10 amendments became known as the Bill of Rights.)

【Section 4】 Listen Efficiently

Linking (2)

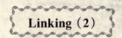

Part 1 Pre-listening Activities

(Class work)

1. Listen to an English song together and note down the words of the song on a piece of paper.

2. Take your partner's note and mark the missing part while we are listening to the song again. (The Greatest Love of All)

3. Discuss the missing parts in class.

Part 2 Listening Task

1. Notice the linking in the case of vowel—to-vowel.

(1) Listen and then practise saying these linked words.

do I　no other　who are　too often

know if　though I　how often　you ought

(2) Listen to the dialogue. Mark the links.

A: How often do I have to do it?

B: You ought to do every exercise once a week.

A: Do I have to do every exercise?

B: Yes, it should take you about two hours. Though I don't suppose it will.

(3) Listen and then practise saying these linked words.

may I　she answers　she is

high up　we ought　the end

(4) Listen to the dialogue and mark the links.

A: Actually, I ought to practise more regularly I suppose.

B: Well, don't worry about it. I often forget myself.

A: Perhaps we ought to try and go together.

(5) Dictation. Listen and complete the dialogue, then mark the links.

A: ①________, Edward.

B: ②________ bad ③________ ④________ exactly

⑤________ place though.

A: ⑥________staying?

B: ⑦________pub ⑧________edge ⑨________.

A: ⑩________what ⑪________ doing ⑫________?

B: ⑬________ actually. This evening there's a ⑭________ on TV, ⑮________ snack ⑯________ town ⑰________ football afterwards.

2. Notice the linking in the case of consonant—to-vowel.

In usual speech, English has a consonant—vowel (CV) pattern. When a word ends in a consonant, that final sound is often moved to the beginning of the next word, *eg* "turn it off" = "tur ni toff", which can maintain the smooth flow of linked words.

Listen to these examples:		
Is he busy?	*sounds like*	Izzybizzy?
take her out		take a route
send her		sender

(1) Listen to these words and then practise saying them.

will I   where I   when I   come on   give up

laugh at   with us   push over   miss (h)im   sing it

(2) Listen to this dialogue and mark the links.

A: Can I help you, sir?

B: Yes, I'm in a rush I'm afraid. Can I have a piece of apple cake please, with ice cream ?

A: Certainly, sir. I'll ask the waiter to come over as soon as possible.

(3) Listen to these words and practice saying them.

where I　when I　pull over　push over

give up　will I　can you　share it

turn on　plan everything

(4) Listen to this dialogue and mark the links.

Example: Switch off the light.

A: Switch off the light, David. It's almost eleven.

B: I'm scared of the dark.. I think I heard a noise. Look over there!

Something on the window ledge is moving.

(5) Listen to these words and then practise saying them.

keep it　skip it　cube of　rob us　flag up

break it　thank us　lend us　said it　stick out

(6) Listen to these groups, concentrating on linking.

① She answers everything.

② Wash all apples.

③ on all our exams

④ Send us out.

⑤ In a way, it's about taxes.

⑥ An athlete must keep practising.

Part 3 Post-listening Activities

1. Study the information below.

(1) A lot of linking occurs with little words beginning with vowels: of, on, in, it, and so on.

eg ① How much is it?

② She's on the phone.

(2) Sometimes, the beginning of the first word is dropped as in the following examples.

eg ① Am I late? Mi late?

② If it's time, I'll go. Fits time

(3) The beginnings of the following sentences have the same pronunciation. The meaning is recognized from the grammar.

eg ① Does it work? Zit work?

② Is it ready yet? Zit ready yet?

2. Read aloud the following sentences with special attention to the articles.

(1) It's a complicated one.

(2) It's an easy one.

(3) I have a little left.

(4) I have little left.

(Note: "A" and "an" are vowels. Because they are linked to the word before, it is very hard to hear them. Sometimes they are not heard at all.)

Unit 6

【Section 1】 Listen Accurately

Forecasting the weather

Task Everyone talks about the weather. Mentioning the weather is a way to greet someone you pass on the street. It's a way to begin a conversation with someone you don't know at a social event. Conversations about the weather are never very long; they are usually only openers to other subjects. A comment about a nice day or a personal complaint about the rain is an easy way to break the ice. Here are some comments about the weather.

Nice day, isn't it?
Looks like rain to me.
I wish this rain would stop.
I can't stand it. It's freezing!
This rain hasn't let up for two weeks. I'm going crazy!
Hot enough for you?
A little on the cool side, isn't it?
It's a perfect day for staying inside!
Isn't it beautiful out today.
Gee, it's slippery out there.

A weatherman gives the forecast on the TV evening news. Write the predicted weather conditions for the weekend on the map next to the name of the city.

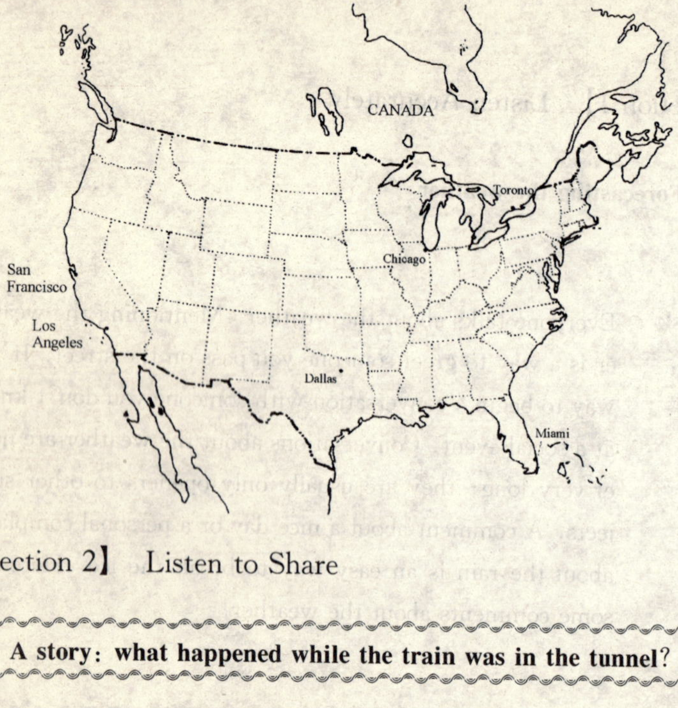

【Section 2】 Listen to Share

A story: what happened while the train was in the tunnel?

Task Listen to the first part of the story. Your teacher will stop it for you. Then discuss these questions with your partner.

(1) How many people are there in one compartment?

(2) What do they look like? Describe each of them to your partner. You may draw a simple picture to show your idea if you like.

(3) What do you think of the sound of the kiss and slap? Who did these?

Now listen to the rest of the story to see whether your guessing is correct or not.

【Section 3】 Listen to Acquire

American government

Joint Session of Congress

Joint sessions of the United States Congress are held infrequently during the course of a regular congressional session. The Senate and House of Representatives only convene jointly when the president wishes to address both houses or when visiting dignitaries give speeches.

US Supreme Court Justices

The framers of the United States Constitution created life-tenures for United States Supreme Court justices. These terms preserve the independence of the court, because members do not need to win political support from voters, nor must they succumb to pressures from the executive and legislative branches of government.

The cabinet of the US government is made up of the administrative heads of the executive departments of the federal government, under the president. Cabinet members are appointed by the president with the approval of the Senate and may be removed by the president either at will or as a result of censure or impeachment by Congress. Unless they resign or are removed, cabinet members serve for the duration of the term or terms of the president who appoints them. The salaries of cabinet officers are fixed by Congress.

Task 1 Listen for specific information—Fill in the blanks.

(1) The forefathers of the nation adopted a ①________ form of government with powers divided between the national and state governments.

(2) The Federal Government takes care of all the matters that are important to ②____________________.

(3) Congress ③__________ the laws, the president ④__________ laws and the Supreme Court ⑤____________ the laws.

(4) The Federal Government has powers to ⑥__________ money, to ⑦ __________ the people, to ⑧ __________ an army, ⑨__________ and ⑩ __________ to defend the nation, and ⑪________ foreign affairs.

(5) The State Governments keep exclusive power over all ⑫____________________.

(6) The States Governments pass laws on ⑬ ________, ⑭ ________, ⑮ ________ and many other important matters.

Task 2 Listen for comprehension—Put the following information into the right place.

Congress, the Senate, the House of Representatives, the President made up of two houses, nine judges of the Supreme Court, with his cabinet, administers the laws, lives in the White House, meet in the Capitol

Three Branches of the Federal Government

the Legislative	the Executive	the Judicial

Task 3 Listen for comprehension—True or False?

(1) The president has the final decision about the interpretation of the laws.

(2) The State Governments take care of important local matters.

【Section 4】 Listen Efficiently

Linking (3)

Part 1 Pre-listening Activities

1. Read aloud the Philosophy of American education in this book.
2. Listen to an American's reading of the same passage.
3. Discuss the difference in his and your reading of the passage.

Part 2 Listening Task

1. Notice the linking in the various cases of consonant to consonant.

When the end of one word has the same sound as the beginning of the next, linking also occurs. This is when the final sound of one word is formed but used for the following word. This makes the first word sound like half a word.

(1) Listen to these words and mark the linking.

Please stop pushing.	He opened the big gate.
Cook it in a deep pot.	He plans to rob both.
She has a black cat.	That's a bad dog.
Put ten in the box.	Where's the red door?

(2) Listen to the following sentences. Connect the words that are linked.

① I wish she knew.

② Who came Mary was absent?

③ Let's stay late tonight.

④ Come Monday, not Tuesday.

2. Notice the linking in various cases of consonant to consonant.

Linking can also occur between two consonants that are similar but not the same. These linked consonants are often formed in similar places in the mouth. It is not practical to memorise all the possible combinations. The best way to learn this linking is to be aware that such linking does occur. The more prepared you are to listen for it, the easier it will be recognised.

Examples:	It's just me.	jus-me t/m
	She was sick.	wa-sick z/s
	What was it?	wha-was t/w
	Sit down.	si-down t/d

(1) Listen to the following sentences. Mark the linking.

① He was sick yesterday.

② Get rid of that.

③ Meet them in the lobby.

④ I've had it with them.

⑤ Let's play it by air.

⑥ As I was saying, now's not a good time.

(2) Listen to the conversation and fill in the blanks with the words you hear.

A: What do you have ①________ way of wrenches?

B: We only carry ②________.

A: Twenty dollars? ③________ just a wrench.

B: You ④________ that'll last a long time, don't you?

A: Yes, ⑤________ spend ⑥________.

B: Actually, this one'll be ⑦________.

I ⑧________ you the sale price today.

A: What kind of discount ⑨________?

B: Twenty-five percent.

A: ⑩________. I'll take it.

3. Notice the linking in the case of the flap.

*When **t** and **d** occur between vowels, they are pronounced as flaps. This sound is similar to a **d**, but it is much faster. The tongue tip touches the tooth-ridge very quickly. (eg butter, idiot.) Linking makes the flap very common. Many words, when spoken in isolation, do not have flaps (eg "what", "to"). However, when linked, a flap can be formed. (eg What else do you want? I'm learning how to do it.) Between a vowel and **l** or **r** the **t** may sound like **d**.*

Idioms can provide good practice for the flap. Listen to the following phrases and repeat after the speaker.

① better off ② put off ③ paid off

④ get over ⑤ out and out ⑥ head on home (on out, on over)

⑦ tired out ⑧ fed up ⑨ get caught up

⑩ get it over with ⑪ have had it with some one

⑫ might as well

4. Listen and fill in the blanks with the words you hear:

(1) A: She has a reputation for being ①________.

B: Don't ②________ it.

(2) A: If you ③________ work more, you'd ④________ ⑤________ A.

B: I have too many other things to get ⑥________

(3) A: Who's going to ⑦________while I'm gone?

B: I'll do the honours.

(4) A: Looks like I found ⑧________ too soon.

B: I ⑨________ to be a surprise.

Part 3 Post-listening Activities

1. Notice the linking in the following phrases and read them.

(1) been no

(2) good deal

(3) felt tired

(4) take this seat

2. Read the following sentences word by word, and read again with a lot of linking occurred.

(1) More rain is expected.

(2) Let Tom make it.

(3) She gave Vick an "A" but Tom a "C".

(Note: Have you noticed that a lot of linking can make a sentence sound much faster?)

Unit 7

【Section 1】 Listen Accurately

Catching planes

BRITISH AIRWAYS

AIR FRANCE

NorthWest Airlines

CATHAY PACIFIC

Delta

UNITED

JAL Japan Airlines

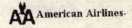

AA American Airlines

Task Listen to the airport announcements and write down the information.

Airline	Flight Number	Departure Gate	Destination
(1) ______	______	______	______
(2) ______	______	______	______
(3) ______	______	______	______
(4) ______	______	______	______
(5) ______	______	______	______
(6) ______	______	______	______
(7) ______	______	______	______
(8) ______	______	______	______

【Section 2】 Listen to Share

A trip to Los Angeles

James Hall has a new job with Orange computers in Philadelphia. He's 23 and just out of college. As part of his training he has to spend six weeks at company headquarters near Los Angeles. It's his first business trip, and he's packing his suitcase. He lives with his parents, and his mother is helping him.

Task Listen to the conversation and write down the things James' mother reminded him of.

____

____

【Section 3】 Listen to Acquire

Parliament in Great Britain

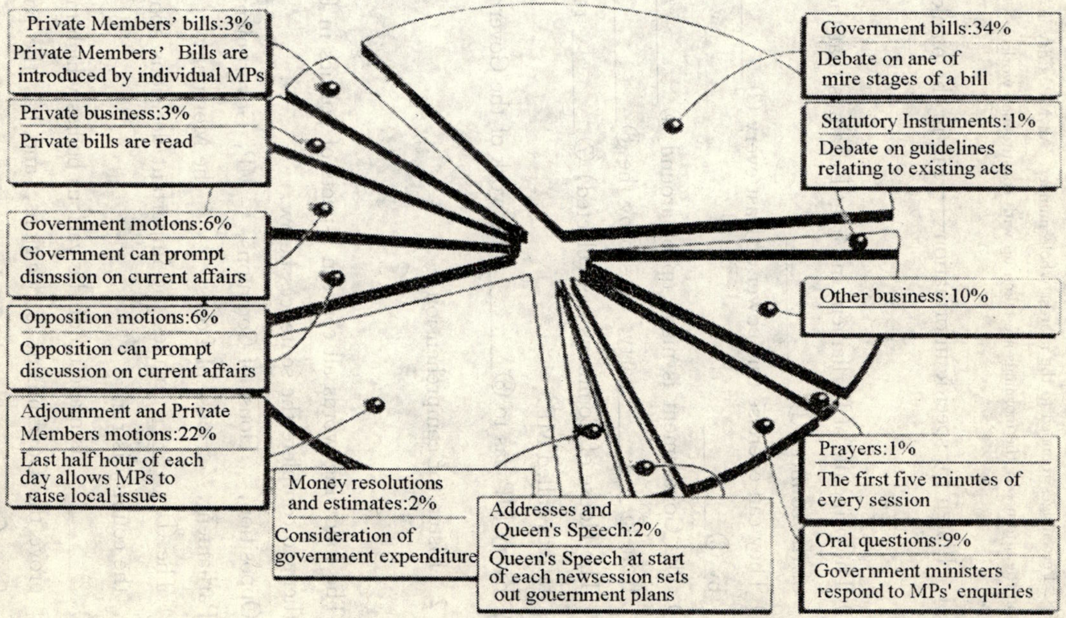
Private Members' bills:3%
Private Members' Bills are introduced by individual MPs
Private business:3%
Private bills are read
Government motlons:6%
Government can prompt disnssion on current affairs
Opposition motions:6%
Opposition can prompt discussion on current affairs
Adjoumment and Private Members motions:22%
Last half hour of each day allows MPs to raise local issues
Money resolutions and estimates:2%
Consideration of government expenditure
Addresses and Queen's Speech:2%
Queen's Speech at start of each newsession sets out gouernment plans
Government bills:34%
Debate on ane of mire stages of a bill
Statutory Instruments:1%
Debate on guidelines relating to existing acts
Other business:10%
Prayers:1%
The first five minutes of every session
Oral questions:9%
Government ministers respond to MPs' enquiries

How MPs spend their time (Division of time in the House of Commons 1987-88. Percentages rounded to the nearest whole number. An MP's day in Parliament begins in the afternoon; the mornings are taken up with constituency work.)

Task 1 Listen for specific information——Fill in the blanks.

(1) The principle of Parliament in Great Britain is that the people of the country ①____________.

(2) They can exercise this power at least every ②________ years by ③________.

(3) The Government is made up of around ④________ people from ⑤________ party, chosen by the ⑥____________.

(4) The House of Commons has (elected) ⑦________ representatives called MP.

(5) Every MP has to ⑧________ the work of the Government.

Task 2 Listen for comprehension.

The following words all concern aspects of politics in Britain. Use them to complete the sentences below.

Opposition, House of Commons, MP, Government,
Parliament, House of Lords, the Monarchy

(1) The ①________ makes the important decisions about how the country is run.

(2) ②________ is made up of the various bodies which must approve the Government's decisions, and has the power to force Government to change its mind.

(3) The three institutions made up of parliament are ③

________, ④________ and ⑤________.

(4) ⑥________ stands for Members of Parliament

(5) The parties which are not part of the government are called the ⑦____________.

【Section 4】 Listen Efficiently

Reduction and contraction (1)

Part 1 Pre-listening Activities

Talk in pairs about the following statements to see if they are true or false according to your experiences:

(1) It's impossible to make out the meaning of what I have listened to if I can't hear every word.

(2) When native speakers talk naturally, quite a lot of sounds that we might expect to hear are not actually pronounced.

(3) As speech becomes more rapid or informal, it becomes more difficult to distinguish individual words.

(4) Vowels in unstressed words are reduced in natural speech.

(5) Reduction is a fundamental characteristic of English and helps explain why written English is so different from spoken English.

Part 2 Listening Task

1. Listen and fill the blanks with the words you hear.

(1) A: ①________another helping?

B: I couldn't eat another ②________.

(2) A: ③________ they ④________?

B: ⑤________.

(3) A: Now ⑥________ happier.

B: It ⑦________.

(4) A: What are you ⑧________ weekend?

B: ⑨________.

(5) A: What do ⑩________ about that?

B: I'm not ⑪________ anything.

(6) A: A hamburger ⑫________ shake.

B: ⑬________ here ⑭________ to go?

(7) A: ⑮________ heard anything yet?

B: No, but ⑯________ an appointment tomorrow.

Maybe I'll find out more ⑰________

(8) A: ⑱________ to work yet?

B: I thought I heard ⑲________ car warming up.

(9) A: ⑳________ made myself clear?

B: Perfectly.

(10) A: ㉑________ finished all the work?

B: All that needs to be done for now.

(11) A: ㉒________ mail come yet?

B: I just saw ㉓________ go by.

(12) A: The lawn needs mowing.

B: As ㉔________ cares.

2. Listen to the recorded extracts of natural speech and complete the dialogues.

(1) A: Will that be cash ①________ charge?

B: Cash—wait, I mean check.

A: Do you have a driver's license ②________ other identification?

B: How about a driver's license ③________ passport?

A: One ④________ the other is OK.

B: Here you are.

(2) A: How ⑤________ keeping since I last saw you?

B: Not so bad. ⑥________, actually, ⑦________ to Sweden for a couple of week ⑧________.

A: And ⑨________no problems since I last saw you?

B: None at all. No, ⑩________ OK.

(3) A: How about another helping?

B: No thanks, I'm stuffed. I've had way more ⑪________ should have.

A: Won't ⑫________ dessert?

B: No, thanks. ⑬________ I'd better not ⑭________ coffee either. I haven't been sleeping so well.

A: ⑮________ been the matter?

B: I'm not sure. ⑯________ headaches.

A: ⑰________ doctor?

B: I don't know ⑱________ for me.

A: It's ⑲________ try.

B: I don't really like the ⑳________, though.

A: Go to mine. I'll give ㉑________ number.

B: Well...

A: ㉒________call. ㉓________ got nothing to lose—except more sleep.

(4) A: Have you ㉔________ your taxes?

B: No. I keep ㉕________ cause I know I'll just ㉖________ more.

A: I owe you a thank. Your advice about ㉗________ invest my money ㉘________paid off. That stock ㉙________ buy took a big drop.

B: I wish I had followed it myself. My finances have really taken ㉚________ these ㉛________. And just as the market was ㉜________ recover...

A: You need the luck of my grandmother. She always ㉝________ the right time.

B: Your grandma? Are you ㉞________?

A: Seriously. She's the most financially secure of the family. And she's done it ㉟________.

B: ㊱________! To think of all the time I've spent studying investments when maybe I should have been ㊲________ your grandmother!

3. Sport Dictation

Listen and see if you can complete this telephone. Write the words exactly as they are spoken. Underline the contractions.

A. Hello, George. This is Sylvia. Can I speak to Jane?

B: Oh, hello, Sylvia. Yes, of course. ①________ with ②________ in a minute. ③________ just come in ④________taking ⑤________ coat off. By the way, John and Barbara called ⑥________ said ⑦________ going ⑧________ Portugal next week. ⑨________ said ⑩________ tell you ⑪________ calling ⑫________ see ⑬________ all right ⑭________ operation.

Part 3 Post-listening Activities

Discuss the summary in the following table with the listening experiences you just have got.

Common reductions and contractions

1. Structure words usually have two forms, *ie* "weak" and "strong". Weak forms are used when the word is not stressed.
2. When weak forms begin with "h", the initial "h" often disappears.
3. Auxiliary verbs can be contracted in natural rapid speech, if unstressed.
4. A syllable containing an unstressed, reduced vowel is often deleted, *eg* p(er)haps, diff(e)rent.
5. Consonants can change or disappear in complex groups of consonants, *ie*:

   "t" and "d": often disappear between two other consonants, *eg* ac(t)s, soun(d)s; they often weaken (or are replaced by a glottal stop) before "p" or "b", *eg* tha(t) book, goo(d) point.

   "n": often sounds like "m" before "p" and "b", *eg* he ca(m) pay, o(m) purpose.

Unit 8

【Section 1】 Listen Accurately

Describing people

Task Listen to some people describing their friends or children and complete the chart.

	Age	Height	Hair
(1)			
(2)			
(3)			
(4)			
(5)			
(6)			

【Section 2】 Listen to Share

Is only always lonely?

Task 1 Before listen to the tape, discuss with your friend about the advantages and disadvantages of being an only child at home.

Task 2 Listen to the tape and answer the questions.

(1) What kind of lifestyle does Zoe King have?

(2) Is Zoe lonely? Why?

(3) What are the two features the speaker mentioned in the end about "only children"?

Task 3 Listen to the tape again and try to complete the paragraph.

Zoe King is ①________ years old. She has got her own ②________, ③________ and ④________. But her parents are ⑤________ than her friends' parents. Although she is the only child, she isn't ⑥________ because there are always ⑦________, ⑧________ and ⑨________ at her home. "Only children are usually ⑩________ for their age. Zoe is quite happy ⑪________".

【Section 3】 Listen to Acquire

Laws in Great Britain

The city of London, capital of Great Britain, is the seat of government. Parliament, seen here, consists of the House of Lords and the House of Commons. Built between 1840 and 1850, the neo-Gothic complex of buildings is still officially called the New Palace of Westminster.

Task 1 Listen for specific information—Fill in the blanks.

(1) Every year, Parliament passes about ①________ laws directly by making Act of Parliament

(2) In this way, it indirectly passes about ②________ additional rules and regulations.

(3) No new law can be passed unless it has completed a number of ③________ in ④________ and ⑤________.

(4) The ⑥________ has to give the Bill the Royal Assent.

(5) There are two main types of Bill—⑦________ and ⑧________.

Task 2 Listen for comprehension—True or False?

(1) The most important job of MPs is to make legislation.

(2) The law-making process is usually time-consuming.

(3) The Government cannot sponsor Public Bills.

(4) Private Member's Bills are often concerned with royal issues. (Note: Britain does not have a written constitution, or set of rules that the Government must obey. Theoretically, the Government has almost unlimited power. However, it can be made to account for its actions. The Prime Minster is also accountable, and twice a week is subjected to detailed questioning in the House of Commons. There are other ways in which the Government's power is restricted by what are called checks and balances. The second chamber, public opinion, the monarch, and top civil servants all play their different roles in influencing or affecting the Government.)

【Section 4】 Listen Efficiently

Reduction and contraction (2)

Part 1 Pre-listening Activities

1. Read the following statements and tell true or false from your own listening experiences:
   (1) Although the principle of some contractions and reductions is fairly easy to understand, it is not at all easy to acquire the habit of recognizing these words in spoken English.
   (2) Our purpose for listening in real life is to recognize the reductions and contractions in spoken English.
2. Study the following part in pairs.
   Structure words can often be pronounced in two different ways: in their strong form or in their weak, reduced form. It is important to know when these forms can and cannot be used. In ordinary, rapid speech such words occur much more frequently in

their weak form than in their strong form.

Look at this example:

① Look at this.

② What are you looking at?

In ①, the vowel in "at" is in its weak or reduced form; but in ② the vowel is strong.

Strong form rules:

These structure words usually have full vowels when they are:

① at the end of a sentence;

② used for emphasis; or

③ used for contrast.

Part 2 Listening Task

1. Listen and then practice these dialogues. Make sure you use the strong and weak forms correctly.

(1) Emphasis on "do" and "that"

A: Which one do you want? This one?

B: No.

A: Well, which one **do** you want?

B: **That** one.

A: Which one?

B: The one that I'm pointing to.

(2) "To" at the end of a sentence

A: Why don't you try to stop?

B: I've tried **to**.

(3) Contrasting "you"

A: I'm surprised you find it so difficult.

B: Well, how did **you** stop?

2. (1) Listen to these sentences. Which version do you hear, A or B?

① A. Did (h) go? B. Did he go?

② A. Is (h)e here? B. Is she here?

③ A. Leave (h)im alone. B. Leave (h)er alone.

④ A. Give (h)im the pen. B. Give me the pen.

⑤ A. Is (h)er work good? B. Is our work good?

(2) Listen to the dialogue and fill in the blanks.

A: When did ①________ go there?

B: I don't know.

A: Who did ②________ talk to ?

B: I don't know.

A: Have you talked to ③________yet?

B: Yes, I have.

A: Did you ask ④________?

B: What?

A: Did you ask ⑤________ who ⑥________ was with?

B: Yes, I did.

A: What did ⑦ ________ say?

B: He said it's none of your business.

(Note: The letter "h" is not omitted when the pronoun is especially emphasised or comes at the beginning of a sentence. *eg*

① Her ideas are brilliant. ② She's good but he's better.)

3. Listen to various kinds of reduction and contractions on word and sentence level.

(1) Disappearing syllables

Sometimes weak vowels in unstressed syllables disappear, giving the impression that the syllable is missing.

Example:　chocolate　choc(o)late

Now listen and mark the sounds that disappear in these words.

① police　② secretary　③ perhaps

④ vegetable　⑤ excuse me　⑥ correct

⑦ potato　⑧ comfortable　⑨ I'm afraid so

(2) Consonant cluster

Consonants can also weaken or disappear, to avoid complex groups of consonants.

Example:　ac(t)s　scripts　scrip(t)s

Now listen and mark the consonants that disappear.

① textbooks　② next week

③ three-fifths　④ he must be ill

⑤ he asked Paul　⑥ she looked back quickly

(3) Nonreleased final consonants

One of the more basic problems in understanding English is non-released final consonants. When p, t, k, b, d, g come at the end of a word, the sound is formed but not released.

Listen to the following sentences. Notice the final sound.

① She acts mad.　② The tape won't stick.

③ A size ten is way too big.　④ He has a broken foot.

⑤ It's store bought.　⑥ He made a mistake.

⑦ Maybe I should.　⑧ I need to take a nap.

Fill in the blanks with the words you hear.

① The party was ________.　② We'll take a ________.

③ Here's my ________.　④ They just got ________.

(4) Ellipsis

You have learned that unstressed syllables are reduced. In

words with more than two syllables, a sound is often completely dropped. This is called ellipsis. Sometimes, the initial syllable can be dropped.

Example:	because	'cause
	about	'bout
	remember	'member
	exactly	'xactly

Before you listen to the following words, try to predict how they will sound with reduced pronunciation. Listen and cross out the dropped syllable:

① generous ② horrible ③ cabinet ④ temperature
⑤ different ⑥ aspirin ⑦ gasoline ⑧ garage
⑨ reference ⑩ favourite

Part 3 Post-listening Activities

1. Summarize the varieties of reductions you have listened to in this lesson.
2. Give some examples from your listening practice after class to demonstrate your summary of reductions in spoken English.

Unit 9

【Section 1】 Listen Accurately

Asking and following directions (1)

Running Errands

Norm has offered to run some errands for his friend,Sandy.On the shoppinglist,write the places where Norm can find the items Label the positions of these places on the map.

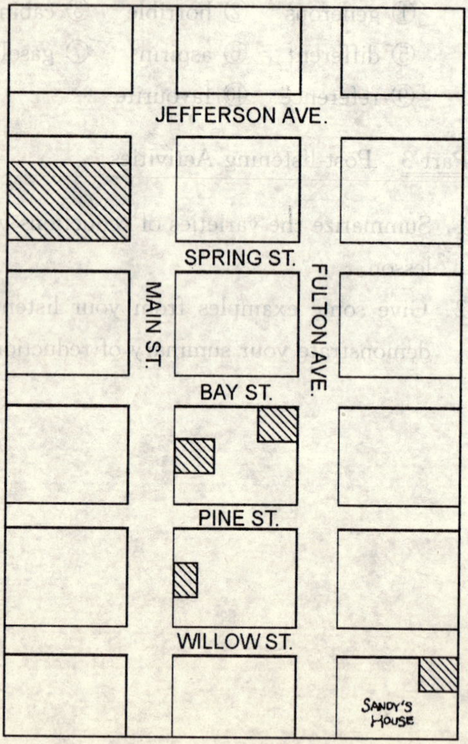

Shopping list

1 loaf bread - Cantor's
3 lbs. apples -
1 lb. cheddar cheese -
5 lb. box rice -
2 lbs. coffee -
1 qt. milk -
6-pack Coke -
large tube toothpaste -

Registered letter -

【Section 2】 Listen to Share

Jigsaw story

Task You will hear sentences from a story (not in their correct order). As you listen, try to take notes for each question and then try to figure out the whole picture of the story.

(1) How did I feel and what did I do?
(2) What did I put on?
(3) What did he do?
(4) Why was I suspicious?
(5) Why didn't "we" want to interfere?
(6) What did my friends do?
(7) What did I try to do?
(8) What was I aware of and what did I think it was?
(9) What did the man hold and where was he?
(10) What did I ask my colleague?

【Section 3】 Listen to Acquire

The family in Great Britain (1)

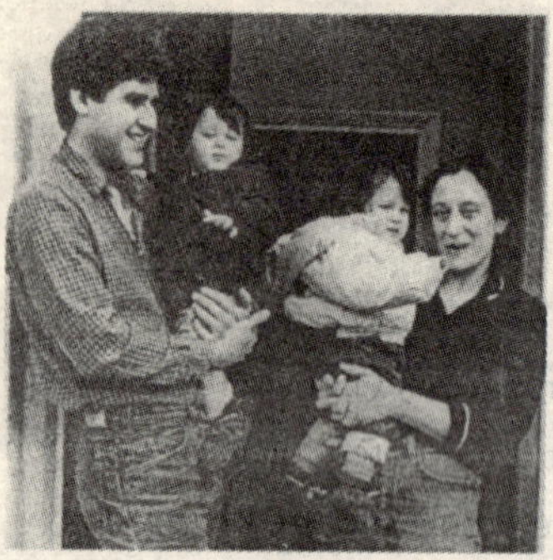

Task 1 Listen for the gist—True or False?

(1) In Great Britain people do not care about family life.

(2) The nuclear family is taken for granted in developed countries.

(3) The family is in a state of crisis in Great Britain.

Task 2 Listen for the details—Fill in the blanks.

(1) People could not do without the ①________ and ②________ of their families.

(2) Politicians often stand for "family values": respects for ③____________, ④________ in marriage, ⑤________ and care for the ⑥____________.

(3) The general type of families, according to ⑦________, are ⑧________ and ⑨________.

(4) The number of ⑩____________ containing a nuclear family is ⑪________ year by year.

(5) Because the family is in ⑫________, some politicians blame ⑬________ problems, such as ⑭________ and ⑮________ on a ⑯________ family life.

(Note: (1) Britain is old-fashioned as regards maternity leave. If they do get maternity leave, women are often worried that, if they do not return to work quickly, they will lose their job and it is often very difficult for them to find another. Paternity leave—time off for the father is rare, although it is becoming common in other European countries. (2) Maternity leave: paid time off for woman who is having or caring for a baby.)

【Section 4】 Listen Efficiently

Reduction and contraction (3)

Part 1 Pre-listening Activities

Discuss the following examples and give more from your own experiences: Some verb forms can be contracted in natural, rapid speech. These are usually auxiliary verbs. Contractions are used to de-emphasise the less important words. This helps to highlight the more important words.

Here are some examples:

Where've (have) you been?

I'd've (would have) come if I'd (had)

I'll (will) do it.

Part 2 Listening Task

1. Listen and fill in the blanks with the words you hear.

(1) A: ①________ like what I fixed?

B: I think ②________ better cooked.

(2) A: ③________ to carpool with someone.

B: ④________ your best bet.

(3) A: ⑤________ a little longer, ⑥________?

B: ⑦________. ⑧________ have dinner—⑨________ cold if I don't hurry.

(4) A: This ⑩________ mess.

B: Given the circumstances, ⑪________ looks pretty good.

Negative auxiliaries are also usually contracted in spoken English, but they are stressed to emphasise the idea of "negation".

Formal	***Informal***
they are not coming	they aren't coming
	they're not coming
we will not be there	we won't be there
	we'll not be there

2. Listen to the recorded dialogues and write down B's responses exactly as you hear them

(1) A: Haven't you finished that report yet?

B: ①________

(2) A: I didn't see Steve yesterday.

B: ②________

(3) A: Do you think Susan has left already?

B: ③________

(4) A: I'm afraid we won't be able to make it this evening.

B: ④________

(Note: When an auxiliary verb comes at the end of a sentence, it cannot be contracted, because the word was placed there for special emphasis. *eg* ① No, I don't think she has. ② Maybe they will.)

3. Listen to Ms Wright's secretary reading back a letter which Ms Wright has dictated to her. After each "bleep", pause the tape and write down what the secretary says.

   When you have finished, listen to the complete letter.

Part 3 Post-listening Activities

1. Discuss the questions below.
   (1) Does the knowledge about the sound of English help with our listening?
   (2) What is the use of knowing something about the change of English sound in natural speech?
2. Share your most favorite English song with the class that demonstrates the simplification of English sound in natural speech.

Unit 10

【Section 1】 Listen Accurately

Asking and following directions (2)

Moving in

A young couple is moving into a small apartment. Write the name of each piece of furniture in its correct position on the floor plan.

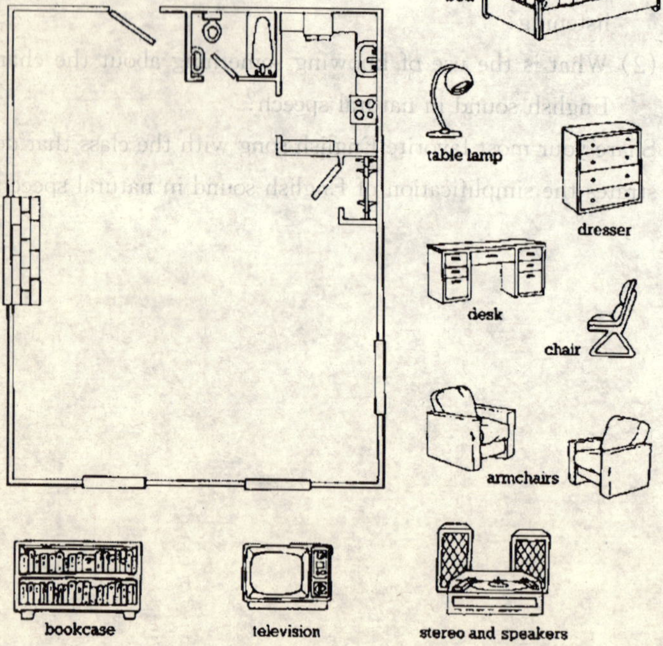

【Section 2】 Listen to Share

The new home

Task 1 Discuss with your partner about the following questions.

(1) Is it necessary to decorate a new home?

(2) Who is going to do the decoration?

(3) What kind of decoration would you prefer?

Task 2 Listen to the conversation and answer these questions.

(1) What recently completed project are the speakers discussing?

(2) Why was the project not as expensive as it might have been?

(3) What was the problem with the kitchen? How was it solved?

(4) Who was the architect?

Task 3 Try to figure out the meanings of the following idioms in this conversation. Then listen to it again and do the matching.

(1) fix up

(2) put our heads together

(3) make do with

(4) hit on

A. develop gradually into the final form

B. manage with less than is usually necessary

C. practice, a rehearsal

D. discuss ideas as part of the creation or problem-solving process

(5) make a breakthrough — E. work together to create or find a solution

(6) kick around — F. lose a creative ability

(7) take shape — G. find a solution after great difficulty

(8) a dry run — H. create in a very imaginative way

(9) dream up — I. decorate; make more attractive or useful

(10) lose one's touch — J. find suddenly

【Section 3】 Listen to Acquire

The family in Great Britain (2)

Task 1 Listen for the gist—True or False?

(1) In Victorian times, the mother was not supposed to go out working.

(2) In the 1990s, there are various ways of family living in Britain.

Task 2 Listen for the details—Fill in the blanks.

(1) In view of "Victorian Values", ①__________ within the family unit was ②__________, and ③__________ standards was ④__________.

(2) The ideal family would go out for an ⑤__________ treat.

(3) The ⑥________ of a golden age is ⑦________ perhaps on

how we think ⑧________ family life should be.

(4) Alternative life ⑨__________, ⑩__________ and ways of ⑪________ children has been socially ⑫________ in the 1990s.

(5) Divorce is no longer seen as ⑬________ and one-parent families are ⑭____________.

(6) People ⑮________ with relationships before ⑯________ themselves to marriage.

【Section 4】 Listen Efficiently

Sound discrimination

Part 1 Pre-listening Activities

1. Listen to the beginning of a story read by the author and try to tell the nationality of the author.

> I was getting along fine with Mama, Papa-Daddy and Uncle Rondo until my sister Stella-Rondo just separated from her husband and came back home again. Mr Whitaker! Of course I went with Mr Whitaker first, when he first appeared here in China Grove, taking "Pose Yourself" photos, and Stella-Rondo broke us up. Told him I was one-sided. Bigger on one side than the other, which is a deliberate, calculated falsehood: I'm the same. Stella-Rondo is exactly twelve months to the day younger than I am and for that reason she's spoiled.

2. Can you tell how many kinds of English you have heard so far?

Part 2 Listening Task

1. Coping with accents

You will hear five speakers with different accents. As you listen, try to match the speakers' accents with the nationalities below. (There are some clues in what the speakers are saying to help you!) Then compare your answers with your partner's.

A. American C. English E. Irish G. South African

B. Australian D. Scottish F. Welsh

Speaker 1 ______________ Speaker 2 ______________

Speaker 3 ______________ Speaker 4 ______________

Speaker 5 ______________

2. Identifying background sounds

Sometimes there are background sounds that can either help with or disturb your listening. You may not need to identify them but they can be useful clues when trying to put what you hear into context.

Listen to ten background sounds and, in groups, suggest where you might hear them.

(The following expressions can help with your descriptions about the sounds)

It sounds...

It sounds like...

It sounds as if...

I can't make out what it is...

It could very well be/couldn't possibly be...

(1) ____

(2) ______________________________

(3) ______________________________

(4) ______________________________

(5) ______________________________

(6) ______________________________

(7) ______________________________

(8) ______________________________

(9) ______________________________

(10) ______________________________

3. Coping with voices against background sounds.

You will hear six people talking over some background sounds. In groups, decide who might be speaking, what the background sound is, where the person might be and what might have happened or might be happening.

	Speaker	Sound	Place	Situation
(1)				
(2)				
(3)				
(4)				
(5)				
(6)				

4. Making a logical guess about context.

Listen to five speakers and try to work out what they might be talking about. Then look for the key words that helped you to guess the context in the transcript.

(1) ____________________

(2) ____________________

(3) ____________________

(4) ____________________

(5) ____________________

Part 3 Post-listening Activities

Discuss the statements below to see whether you agree on them.

- People speak English with different accents but they are never unintelligible.
- You will not be put off by accents if you have been exposed to a variety of accents.
- It is important to be able to identify various kinds of accents if you want to understand spoken English.

Unit 11

【Section 1】 Listen Accurately

Finding out about a course

Task A student phones a college office for information about courses. Write down the answers to her questions.

Things to do--Aug. 29
Call Clarkson College about computer programming courses--TODAY!
Name of course:
Which evening(s)?
Time:
Dates: Starts--
Ends--
Cost:
Registration
When:
Where:
What to bring:

【Section 2】 Listen to Share

School decision

Task 1 Discuss with your partner about the following questions.

(1) Do you have to choose courses in your study?

(2) Would you like to have some optional courses so that you can decide what to take by yourself?

(3) What kind of courses do you like best?

Task 2 Listen to the conversation and answer the questions.

(1) Why hasn't the man registered for his courses yet?

(2) What courses is he considering? What courses does he refuse to consider?

(3) Why doesn't he want to ask the advisor to help him choose?

Task 3 Guess the meanings of the following idioms in this conversation. Listen to it again and try the matching.

(1) out of the question	A. be the decision of someone
(2) take into account	B. certainly, of course
(3) turned him down	C. examine carefully, study
(4) draw the line at	D. have a role in decision-making
(5) looked over	E. consider when making a decision
(6) is up to you	F. absolutely impossible
(7) on second thought	G. change a decision or agreement

that has already been made; remove support for a decision

(8) back out of — H. refuse; reject

(9) by all means — I. not accept

(10) have a voice in — J. change a decision after thinking about it again.

【Section 3】 Listen to Acquire

Some of the problems facing learners of English

Words and expressions
medium, category, psychological, linguistic, academic accommodation, a variety of accents

Task 1 Listen for the gist—Questions for listening.

(1) What are the three problems facing learners of English?

(2) Of the three, which is the focus of the lecture?

(3) How many pieces of advice about speaking are provided here?

Task 2 Listen for the details—True or False?

(1) The speaker says he will not spend a long time talking about the psychological and cultural problems.

(2) There are really only three reasons for having difficulty in understanding people.

(3) The speaker says that students speak with a variety of accents.

(4) In order to understand English people better, perhaps the most important thing for a student to do is to listen to the radio and TV.

(5) The advice given on how to improve spoken English will seem difficult to follow.

Task 3 Follow-up activity

Listen to the lecture again and discuss the following questions in pairs.

(1) Which of the categories of problems mentioned have you personally experienced? To what degree?

(2) Which category of problems do you anticipate facing in the future?

(3) Have you tried any of the ways of overcoming the linguistic difficulties suggested by the lecturer? With what degree of success?

(4) Have you got any further advice to offer your fellow students?

【Section 4】 Listen Efficiently

Rhythm

Part 1 Pre-listening Activities

1. Study the following information about English rhythm.

(1) Rhythm in English is not just something extra, added to the

basic sequence of consonants and vowels, it is the guide to the structure of information in the spoken message.

(2) The most important feature of English rhythm is that the syllables are not equal in duration.

(3) The rhythm of English speech depends on the alternation of stressed and unstressed syllables, which is important for understanding.

2. Read aloud the following examples.

Examples: *above* *return* *select*

Stressed syllables are long. Unstressed syllables are usually short. A long syllable is usually surrounded by shorter syllables.

Examples:	Peter	banana
	an apple	in London
	absolute	Have some fruit
	impossible	it's possible

Part 2 Listening Task

1. Listen and count the syllable of each word, and then practice the rhythm of the following words.

administration	clarification	identification	internationalization
examination	justification	reinterpretation	
simplification		reunification	

2. Listen and match the rhythm of the phrases in the right-hand column with the rhythm of the words in the left-hand column, and then practise saying them in the correct order. Notice that a word said by itself is like a small phrase; it must have all the rhythm and stress of a phrase.

Example: *simplification* →	*such a reduction*
computerisation	the action
interruption	he works at the station
addition	another option
clarification	shocked the nation
communication	who did she mention

3. Listen and then practise saying these sentences. Notice that when two or more stressed syllables come together, length is added to each syllable, which makes the speech sound stronger.

Get out!	Birds don't eat grass.
Please come here.	Put that down now.
Don't talk nonsense.	Bring hot water.

4. You will hear twelve sentences. Write down the number of the sentences with a series of stressed syllables in the left column and that of the ones made of syllables of different lengths in the right column.

Regular syllable length (all stressed syllables)	Irregular syllable length (stressed and unstressed syllables)
____________	____________
____________	____________

Listen again to write down the entire sentences one by one, and then read aloud.

(1) ______________________________

(2) ______________________________

(3) ______________________________

(4) ______________________________

(5) ______________________________

(6) ______________________________

(7) ____

(8) ____

(9) ____

(10) ____

(11) ____

(12) ____

5. (1) Listen and repeat the following lines. Notice the last three words in this sentence are dramatically slowed down because there are three long syllables together.

go right now

if you *go right now*

You might get there in time if you *go right now*

in time

get there *in time*

you might get there *in time*

Now listen and repeat the following sentences Make sure you stress the last three syllables in the same way.

The government intends to stop all strikes.

The robbers were finally arrested today after a ten-week search.

6. Listen to the following limerick and then practice the rhythm.

A STUdent was SENT to TaCOma
InTENding to EARN a diPLOma.
He SAID, "With the RAIN,
I don't WANT to remain.
I THINK I'd preFER OklaHOma."

Part 3 Post-listening Activities

1. Read the following lines of a poem aloud.

   Whose woods these are I think I know
   His house is in the village though;
   He will not see me stopping here
   To watch his woods fill up with snow.

2. Tell the name of the poem and the writer of the poem.
3. Find out the rest of the poem and share with the class.

Unit 12

【Section 1】 Listen Accurately

Telephone messages

Task In daily life, people often need to take telephone messages. So it is very important to know what should be taken down. A woman is trying to phone her friend. Put a check (√) next to the picture that best describes the message that she leaves.

1

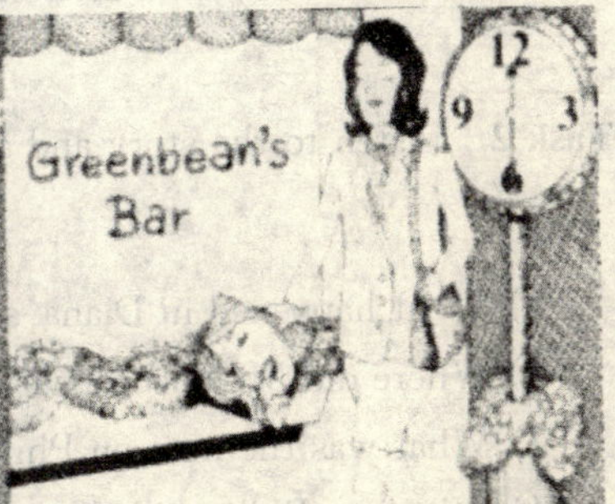

2

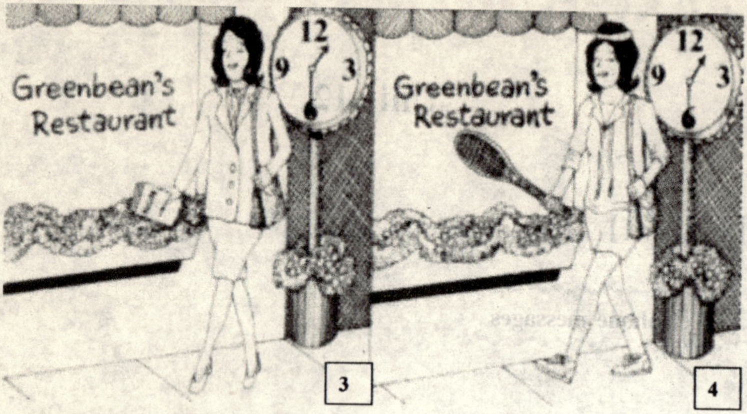

【Section 2】 Listen to Share

A dangerous woman?

Task 1 Before you listen to the tape, discuss with your partner about what kind of woman is dangerous.

Task 2 Listen to the story and answer the following questions.

(1) What happened in Diana's home?

(2) Where did Mr Spenser visit first after he accepted the case?

(3) What was the note on Philip's desk about?

(4) Why was Philip killed?

(5) Why Diana was suspected by the police? How did this happen to her?

Task 3 Check your comprehension of the story—True or False?

(1) It was a very cold day in New York.
(2) When a beautiful woman came, Spensor did nothing.
(3) Diana put ten thousand dollars on Spensor's desk.
(4) Yesterday evening Diana arrived home early.
(5) Diana felt very tired last night and she fell asleep immediately.
(6) Philip didn't have any friends.
(7) Mr Spensor drove to Divine's house and a man answered the door.
(8) In the end, Divine and Lomax were shot to death.

【Section 3】 Listen to Acquire

Attitude towards the learning of vocabulary

Words and expressions
post-graduate, contrary to, emerge, equivalent, principle, investigation, observation, imitation

Task 1 Listen for the gist—Questions for listening.

(1) How were the results of a recent investigation of students' attitude towards vocabulary learning?
(2) Please list the three wrong attitudes mentioned in the lecture.

(3) What is the best way to increase one's vocabulary?

Task 2 Listen for the details—True or False?

(1) There has recently been an investigation into the attitudes of undergraduate science students towards language learning.

(2) The use of vocabulary lists may encourage a student to think that nearly every word in English has just one meaning.

(3) Every word in English has an exact translational equivalent in the student's native language.

(4) Translation machines failed because they worked on the principle of a one word for one word translation process.

(5) To use words correctly it is not enough to learn only their meanings.

Task 3 Follow-up activity

Listen to the lecture again and discuss the following questions in pairs.

(1) Before the talk, did you share any of the misconceptions found to exist among the non-native English-speaking postgraduate science students questioned? If so, which?

(2) The lecturer offers two possible reasons for the first misconception. Which in your experience / opinion is the more likely ? Give reasons.

(3) Can you think of any words in your first language which illustrate the problematic nature of translation?

(4) The lecturer suggests three ways of increasing one's vocabu-

lary in a foreign language. Have you developed any additional strategies which you could recommend to your fellow students?

【Section 4】 Listen Efficiently

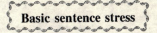

Basic sentence stress

Part 1 Pre-listening Activities

1. Tell True or False of the statements below.
   (1) English rhythm is based not only on word stress but also on sentence stress.
   (2) If non-native speakers of English are not aware of the basis of English rhythm, they will often miss important signals in listening comprehension.
2. Read the table below.

Basic sentence stress				
Content words (stressed)				
nouns (bike)	main verbs (send)	negative auxiliaries (don't, can't)	adverbs (quickly)	adjectives (big)
Structure words (not stressed)				
pronouns (he, she)	prepositions (on, at)	articles (a, the)	"to be" verbs (is, was)	
conjunctions (and, but)	auxiliary verbs (can, do, will)			

Part 2 Listening Task

1. Listen and then underline the content words in the following sentences.

   (1) Can I have a coffee and a cup of tea, please?

   (2) Would you like another one?

   (3) Thanks for a lovely meal.

   (4) Sorry but I can't come on Monday because I'm working late.

   (5) I've never been to a car rally.

   (6) I usually visit my parents on Tuesdays.

2. Listen to this dialogue and underline the content words.

   A: Are you ready?

   B: Not quite.

   A: Put your coat on.

   B: Just a minute. Don't rush me.

3. Listen to these telephone messages for Chris from his boss. Then write down the messages as notes on the message pad. Write only the essential information, the content words.

Telephone Message From: ________________ To:
Messages (1) ________________ (2) ________________ (3) ________________ (4) ________________

4. Listen to the recorded excerpt of natural speech and write down exactly what you hear.

A: ____

____

____

B: ____

____

____

5. Listen to the beginning of this song by Laurie Anderson. Underline the content words and then practise saying it while you listen.

Good evening. This is your Captain.

We are about to attempt a crash landing.

Please extinguish all cigarettes.

Place your tray tables in their upright, locked position.

Your Captain says: Put your head on your knees.

Your Captain says: Put your head in your hands.

Part 3 Post-listening Activities

Fill in the blanks below.

(1) In most sentences there are two types of words: __________.

(2) ____________ normally carry the most information and they are often emphasised.

(3) ______________ do not carry so much information and they are not normally emphasised.

Unit 13

【Section 1】 Listen Accurately

Eating out

Task Listen to the two dialogues and put a tick beside the food these two guests chose.

Menu

Appetizers			
Vegetable soup	4.50		
House salad	3.75		
Main dishes			
Steak with fries	18.00		
Roast chicken	9.95		
Spaghetti with meat sauce	11.00		
Desserts			
Apple pie	3.75		
Ice cream	2.75		
Drinks			
Tea	1.50	Soda	1.75
Coffee	1.50	Juice	2.00

Menu

Appetizers			
Soup of the day	4.50		
Salad	5.00		
Main dishes			
Vegetarian plate	9.50		
Grilled fish with broccoli or peas	13.00		
Desserts			
Chocolate cake	3.75		
Ice cream	2.75		
Drinks			
Iced Tea	1.50	Soda	1.75
Coffee	1.50	Juice	2.00

【Section 2】 Listen to Share

An arranged marriage

You will hear an interview with a member of the Sikh community in Britain, who talks about the idea of arranged marriage.

Task 1 Before you listen, work with your partner and write down any questions you would like to ask him about arranged marriage.

Task 2 Listen to the tape and check out how many of your questions have been answered. Try to answer the following questions.

(1) Are partners dragged into a marriage in "my" culture?

(2) How was "my marriage" arranged? Whose idea was it?

(3) What would be the important thing in deciding on a suitable partner for a person?

(4) Many people believe that it's not the parents who are getting married, it's the children who are getting married so the children should decide. What do "I" think about this?

(5) Can an arranged marriage be called off? How?

Task 3 In the following summary there are some factual mistakes. Correct the mistakes.

Gurmit and I didn't know each other before our marriage. My mother approached his father and both of them decided the marriage. We are of similar age and have similar hobbies and outlooks, so it's worked very well.

Before any couple is introduced to each other, the parents will do a fair amount of research about the general behaviour, the education background. They don't care too much about the family's wealth and their standing in the society.

I think parents have had a better experience than the children. No parent wants to see their children's marriage break up. They would choose a partner for their children and once it is arranged their children can't say no and can't call off the arrangement.

I think love comes out of a relationship. Once a relationship starts, you have to use it to your benefit, you have to give and take and to be tolerant.

【Section 3】 Listen to Acquire

Effective reading

Words and expressions contain, invaluable, put forward, in great detail, adopt, overview, skimming, put into practice, strategy, efficiently

Task 1 Listen for the gist—Questions for listening.

(1) By doing what can students make their reading more effective?

(2) What is, perhaps, the most useful part of their reading strategy?

(3) How many kinds of reading speed are mentioned here? What are they?

Task 2 Listen for the details—True or False?

(1) When a teacher recommends a book he never recommends the whole book.

(2) An overview of the contents of a book can be obtained by reading the index.

(3) The only advantage of a student making notes as he reads is that they provide him with a summary.

(4) A student should read as carefully as possible because he has a lot to read in a short time.

(5) A student's slowest reading speed is used for obtaining a general idea of the reading material.

Task 3 Follow-up activity

A speaker often wishes to comment on the content of what he is saying. This is often done by means of sentence adverb placed at the beginning of a sentence, which can serve as a signal to help listeners with their prediction of the meaning of the speaker. *eg* Unfortunately, when many students pick up a book to read they tend to have no particular purpose in mind. In the sentences below the comment adverb is underlined. Choose the appropriate part of the sentence to follow it:

(1) Tom studied very hard. Surprisingly,

A. he passed his exams.

B. he was not lazy.

C. he failed his exams.

(2) John was late for the appointment. Fortunately,

A. he had forgotten the time.

B. his tutor was still waiting.

C. his tutor was very angry.

(3) His application arrived too late. Officially,

A. it could not be accepted.

B. it did not matter.

C. it could be considered.

(4) His experiment contained a few minor errors. Basically, however,

A. it was unreliable.

B. it was reliable.

C. it was inaccurate.

【Section 4】 Listen Efficiently

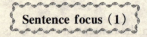

Sentence focus (1)

Part 1 Pre-listening Activities

1. Answer the following questions from your listening experience.

(1) What is the basic stress pattern used by native speakers of English in speech?

(2) How can speakers highlight the information they want to emphasize?

2. Study the basic pattern of sentence focus

(1) When a conversation begins, the focus is usually on the last content word.

Examples:

What's the matter?   Where are you going?

Put the coffee in it.

(2) The focus of a sentence can be broad.

Examples:

I've lost my keys.

My flight leaves at 11:30 on Tuesday the sixth.

He's stolen my bag.

(The focus is on more than one word, or a phrase, but the centre of focus is on the last content word, *ie* "bag".)

(3) The focus can be narrow.

Examples:

Here they are!   I'm not ready.   Who's stolen your bag?

(The focus is on one word.)

Part 2 Listening Task

1. Listen to these sentences and underline the focus words.

(1) The film was fantastic!

(2) Are you coming to the party on Saturday?

(3) Can you give it to him?

(4) I think I left it in the bedroom.

2. Listen to the questions and answer them as quickly as possible. The answers can be one or two words, and they should respond to the focus word in the question.

(1) ____________________

(2) ____________________

(3) ____________________

(4) ____________________

(5) ____________________

(6) ____________________

3. Listen to these dialogues and underline the focus words, then practise saying them using the same focus pattern.

(1) A: I've lost my hat. (basic stress pattern: the content word is focused)

B: What kind of hat? ("hat" is now an old idea; "kind" is the new focus)

A: It was a sun hat.

B: What colour sun hat?

A: It was white. White with stripes.

B: There was a white hat with stripes in the car.

A: Which car?

B: The one I sold.

(2) A: Hello. What's new?

B: Nothing much. What's new with you?

A: I'm going to the States.

B: East coast or West coast?

A: West. I want to visit San Francisco.

(3) A: Are you going on holiday?

B: No. I'm going to study.

A: Study what? Maths or English?

B: Neither. I'm sick of maths and English. I'm going to study engineering. Electronic engineering.

4. Listen to the following conversation and notice the changes in focus.

(1) A: What are you doing?

B: I came to see Peter.

A: Well, Peter's not here.

B: I can see he's not here. Where is he?

A: I don't know where he is.

B: Not very friendly, are you?

A: Neither are you.

(2) A: Do you think American food's expensive?

B: Not really.

A: Well, I think it's expensive.

B: That's because you eat in restaurants.

A: Where do you eat?

B: At home.

A: I didn't know you could cook.

B: Well, actually I can't. I just eat bread and Coke.

A: That's awfully!

B: No, it isn't. I like bread and Coke.

A: You're crazy!

Part 3 Post-listening Activities

1. Can you find out something useful to listening by reading the following statements?

(1) Native speakers can focus the listener's attention on the parts of the message that are most important in a particular context.

(2) The sentence focus helps the listener relate something to what has been said before and to predict what it is likely to be said next.

(3) Which words are focused depends on which words the speaker considers important for the listener to notice.

2. Read the following statements to see whether you agree or disagree.

(1) Learning to hear sentence focus is difficult but important because it helps make a major step forward in listening comprehension.

(2) If we listen without some awareness of sentence focus, it is likely to miss spoken signals of contrast with something said or assumed previously.

Unit 14

【Section 1】 Listen Accurately

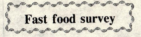

Fast food survey

Task 1 Look at the answers and try to think of a way to ask people appropriate questions. Try it out with your partner.

(1) I usually have pizzas.
(2) I eat fast food everyday.
(3) I think fast food is very convenient.

Task 2 Now you will hear a market researcher asking someone questions about fast food. Listen to the tape and try to finish the questionnaire.

1. Do you ever eat fast food?
   □ Yes　　No
2. What kind of fast food do you normally eat?
   1. ________　　2. ________
   3. ________　　4. ________
3. How often do you eat fast food?
   □ every day　□ more than once a week　□ less than once a week

4. What time of day do you eat fast food?

   □ in the morning　　□ in the afternoon

   □ around midday　　in the evening

5. Do you eat fast food as:

   □ a main meal?　　□ a snack between meals?

6. Which of these statements about fast food do you think are true?
   (*Mark the scale*: *3 = Yes*, *2 = Maybe/Not sure*, *1 = No*)

	3	2	1
It's convenient.			
It tastes good.			
It's good for you.			
It's an expensive way of eating.			
It creates litter.			

【Section 2】 Listen to Share

Caring for nature and culture

Task 1　Before listen to the tape, please discuss with your partner.

(1) Why is it important to protect nature?

(2) What kind of things should we protect?

(3) How can we protect them?

Listen to the first conversation and drop down a few lines about the issues mentioned above.

Task 2 Before listen to the tape, read the following list and decide why they are listed together.

CHINA

1987 The Great Wall

1987 Mount Taishan

1987 Imperial Palace of the Ming and Qing Dynasties

1987 Mogao Caves

1987 Mausoleum of the First Qin Emporer

1987 Peking Man Site at Zhoukoudian

1990 Mount Huangshan

1992 Jiuzhaigou Valley Scenic and Historic Interest Area

1992 Huanglong Scenic and Historic Interest Area

1992 Wulingyuan Scenic and Historic Interest Area

1994 The Mountain Resort and its Outlying Temples, Chengde

1994 Temple and Cemetery of Confucius, and the Kong Family Mansion in Qufu

1994 Ancient Building Complex in the Wudang Mountains

1994, 2000 Potala Palace and the Jokhang Temple Monastery, Lhasa

1996 Lushan National Park

1996 Mount Emei and Leshan Giant Buddha

1997 Old Town of Lijiang

1997 Ancient City of Ping Yao

1997, 2000 Classical Gardens of Suzhou

1998 Summer Palace, an Imperial Garden in Beijing

1998 Temple of Heaven—an Imperial Sacrificial Altar in Beijing

1999 Mount Wuyi

1999 Dazu Rock Carvings

2000 Mount Qincheng and the Dujiangyan Irrigation System

2000 Ancient Villages in Southern Anhui—Xidi and Hongcun

2000 Longmen Grottoes

2000 Imperial Tombs of the Ming and Qing Dynasties

Now listen to the second conversation and write down the questions that they ask when they decide which places should belong to the World Heritage Organization.

(1) ____________________

(2) ____________________

(3) ____________________

(4) ____________________

【Section 3】 Listen to Acquire

Problems of writing in a foreign language

Words and expressions			
analyze,	distinguish,	a breakdown in communication,	
refer to,	interfere with,	feature,	prominently

Task 1 Listen for the gist—Questions for listening.

(1) Is writing the most difficult skill for learners of English to

master?

(2) What are the three types of errors analyzed here?

Task 2 Listen for the details—True or False?

(1) Native speakers, because they are fluent in English, find few problems in writing in their special subjects.

(2) The three main types of errors in writing are more or less equal importance.

(3) Word by word translation often results in un-English sentences.

(4) Choosing a wrong verb tense will normally cause a breakdown in meaning.

(5) The use of a word such as "terrific" in academic writing is an example of an error in style and usage.

Task 3 Follow-up activity

Listen to the lecture again and discuss the following questions in pairs:

(1) Which of the problems described by the lecturer have you encountered when writing in English?

(2) Have you experienced any other difficulties? If so, what are they?

List the five most serious problems identified above in order of severity, beginning with what you consider to be your greatest source of difficulty when writing in English.

Problem	Frequency of occurrence
(1)	
(2)	
(3)	
(4)	
(5)	

【Section 4】 Listen Efficiently

Sentence focus (2)

Part 1 Pre-listening Activities

1. What do people usually do in conversations? Write more on the lines below.

   (1) exchange information or ideas

   (2) state or deny a fact strongly

   (3) give or disagree with an opinion

   (4) ______________________________

   (5) ______________________________

   (6) ______________________________

2. There are different ways of manipulating language to express these various meanings. One way of giving special meaning is by using stress to give contrastive focus. Read some functions of sentence focus in the following examples:

(1) Correcting information

Speakers can focus words to contradict or deny any idea in a previous sentence. This pattern is common when speakers want to correct information.

Example:

A: Here you are. Two teas and a coffee.

B: But we didn't want two teas. We want one.

(2) Checking information

Speakers can focus words to query a previous speaker's sentence.

Example:

A: It took me two hours to get to work this morning.

B: Two hours?

Part 2 Listening Task

1. Listen to this dialogue and then practise it. Make sure you emphasise the focus.

   A: Good morning. May I help you?

   B: Yes, I'd like to speak to Mr Williams, please.

   A: What's your name, please?

   B: John Ribble.

   A: Mr Williams. There's a Mr Riddle to see you.

   B: Excuse me not Riddle, Ribble.

   A: Oh, sorry. There's a Mr Ribble to see you, Mr Williams.

2. Read the dialogue and see if you can mark the focus words.

   (C for Customer, W for Waiter)

   C: Can I have one cheese sandwich and two ham rolls, please?

   W: That's one ham sandwich . . .

C: No, one cheese sandwich.

W: Sorry, that's one cheese sandwich and two ham sandwiches.

C: No, two ham rolls.

W: Right... You did want two cheese sandwiches, didn't you?

C: No, I didn't. Just one.

W: Oh. I think I'd better write this down.

Now listen to the dialogue and check the focus.

(Notice how the focus in a question shows what the person wants to know. The answer speakers give depends on the word that had the most emphasis in the question.)

3. Listen to the policeman asking a woman about a bank robbery. Notice which word he focuses on in each sentence. After each "bleep" choose the appropriate reply and put a cross by it.

Example:

Policeman: Excuse me, madam, but were you in the bank on Friday?

Reply: A. No, but my sister was. ___+___

B. No, but I was near it. ______

(1) Reply: A. No, on Thursday.

B. Yes, every Friday.

(2) Reply: A. No, but I heard them.

B. No, I just saw the guards.

(3) Reply: A. No, I screamed.

B. No, someone else did.

(4) Reply: A. No, I think there were two.

B. No, I think there was a woman.

4. Now try and give a suitable response to question each of the sentences you hear.

(1) A: I didn't go on Friday.

B: ________________________________

(2) A: He's been promoted.

B: ________________________________

(3) A: I found your keys in the kitchen.

B: ________________________________

(4) A: Have you seen my purse anywhere?

B: ________________________________

(5) A: The France / Scotland match has been postponed.

B: ________________________________

5. Shifting the focus can affect the listener's interpretation of the message, so it is important to recognise the most emphasised word.

Example :

I thought it was going to rain. (but it didn't)

I thought it was going to rain. (and it did)

Listen to the conversation between Paul and Barbara. Is Barbara confirming what actually happened or querying something? Put a cross in the appropriate column.

	Querying	Confirming
(1) I thought you'd have a nice time.	______	______
(2) I thought you were going to Spain.	______	______
(3) But I thought you were going with Maria	______	______
(4) I rather thought there might be problems.	______	______
(5) I thought you'd been there.	______	______

(6) I thought you spoke Italian. ________

____

(7) I thought you were coming to my party on Saturday. ________ ________

Part 3　Post-listening Activities

1. Listen and Underline the focus in B's answers below. Then read the dialogues in pairs, with special attention to B's part.

(1) A: Oh, I'll have to go and get the paper.
B: I'll get it for you.

(2) A: When can I collect the photographs?
B: I'm afraid they won't be ready until Tuesday.

(3) A: I'm glad you're coming on Friday.
B: But I can't come.

2. Listen and underline the focus words. Then read the dialogue, noticing the contrastive focus.

(1) A: Peter is funny.
B: He isn't funny. He's strange.

(2) A: So the number is 35487.
B: No, it's 35187.

(3) A: That's $ 3.15 together.
B: $ 3.50?
A: No, $3.15.

Unit 15

【Section 1】 Listen Accurately

Palm reading

Task Listen to two people's comments about a person's palm. Please decide which statements they agree with and put an "A" in their own columns.

About his character	Speaker 1	Speaker 2
He has a strong character.		
He's unsure of himself.		
He's a practical person.		
He's an imaginative person.		
About his past		
He was probably ill when he was younger.		
He wasn't sure what to do when he was younger.		
About his future		
He'll continue in the same job.		
He'll have important relationships with two women.		
He'll retire early.		

【Section 2】 Listen to Share

A ghost story

Task 1 You will hear two friends, Stephanie and Rob, talking about Stephanie's experiences with strange powers whilst living in an old house in London. Listen to the first part of the story and take notes under each heading.

Stephanie's first encounters with the spirit	The night she first saw the spirit	The night the pictures fell off the wall	The things you think going to happen next

Task 2 This is the second part of the story. After you listen to it try to do the exercises.

(1) How did Stephanie's husband communicate with the spirit?

(2) Write down the questions he asked.

____

____

____

(3) Describe the spirit.

It was a ①________. He lived there when ②________, it had been ③________ for him in the ④________, and in fact that it had been ⑤________, and that's why he came there. He was really quite a ⑥________ spirit, and he was just ⑦________ the house and had been all the time, and he was ⑧________ in the house.

(4) Do you believe Stephanie's story? If you don't, how can it be explained?

(5) How did Stephanie feel about the ghost? Would you have felt the same?

(6) Do you know any similar stories? If so, please share them with your partner.

【Section 3】 Listen to Acquire

The importance of questions

Words and expressions
concentrate on, grammatical, consequently appropriate, preface, predictable

Task 1 Listen for the gist—Questions for listening.

(1) What is important in group discussion?

(2) Why does sometimes the teacher agree or disagree with his students instead of providing answers for them?

(3) What can you do if you want a teacher to give suitable answers?

Task 2 Listen for the details—True or False?

(1) It is advisable for a student to focus all his attention on the subject matter when he is involved in a discussion.

(2) A student who has learned to use question forms correctly has

no further problems with asking questions.

(3) The teacher must make certain that he is clear about the exact reference of a student's question.

(4) The use of an appropriate background statement before a question helps to make an inquiry more specific.

(5) A teacher is not normally in a position to give suitable answers to questions unless they are precise.

Task 3 Follow-up activity

The lecture emphasized the importance of asking precise questions. The table below summarizes ways in which questions may be asked in order to get a repetition or an explanation of some item not previously understood. Look carefully at the table. Remember that each question should begin with a polite request: "Excuse me, please could you..." Practice it in pairs.

Required action	Required item	Time reference	Topic reference	Mode of repetition
repeat explain	the last sentence			more clearly?
	the reference you made what you said	just now a minute ago at the beginning	about: cost inflation(?) state planning(?)	more loudly? more slowly?
explain	what you meant the reference		the percentage involved(?) the rate of illiteracy (?)	
Write	the author's name you mentioned the book title you gave			on the blackboard?

【Section 4】 Listen Efficiently

Functions of intonation (1)

Part 1 Pre-listening Activities

1. Read the following and underline the importance of intonation in spoken English.

> It has been shown in the researches of some linguists that intonation is a feature of the spoken language. It consists of the continuous changing of the pitch of a speaker's voice to express meanings. People can mean different things by using the same group of words, arranged in the same order, but saying them in different ways. Intonation as a system is very complex. Within limited time, only some of its functions can be shown here to enable us to become aware of and sensitive to the way English speakers use intonation in natural speech.

2. Just as what you did with the importance of intonation in the exercise above, the speakers of English highlight some of their words to make them most significant in conversations. A highlighted word in spoken English sounds noticeable because it contains a prominent syllable that is a slightly raised pitch.

Part 2 Listening Task

1. (1) Listen to the conversation and try to answer the questions.

① What is Alan trying to do?

② Why does he find it so difficult?

③ How does Louise react to his attempt?

(2) Now listen to this short excerpt from the conversation. In the transcript below underline the words that you think are most noticeable.

Alan: Turn slightly towards me.

Your head slightly towards me.

Louise: Right?

Alan: No—only slightly towards me.

Compare your transcript with a partner. Try to say why the same word is sometimes highlighted and sometimes not.

(3) Listen to the conversation again.

2. (1) Listen to this conversation between John and Lisa and then answer the questions.

① What has Samantha told Lisa on the phone?

② What is the special significance of red roses?

③ What are the two different meanings John and Lisa give to "poor guy"?

(2) Listen to the first part of the conversation again.

① Identify any phrase(s) which you hear repeated. In the transcript which follows, underline the words which you think the speaker highlighted.

② Look carefully at the contexts of the phrases and try to explain why the highlighting has changed.

Lisa: That was Samantha on the phone. Honestly, I don't know how she does it.

John: Ah... Samantha. What's she done now?

Lisa: Nothing, really. That's what's amazing. But somebody has sent her a dozen roses.

John: A dozen what?

Lisa: ... a dozen roses.

John: Roses ... mmm, I say! ... and at this time of year ...

Lisa: Yes. And a dozen roses. He must be keen.

John: Is it her birthday of something?

Lisa: No, and what's more they were red roses.

John: Now ... a dozen red roses. You know what that means?

(3) Now listen to the second part of the conversation and do the same again.

Lisa: Yes. I know what you're going to say.

John: It means he's not just keen. He's in love with her.

Lisa: I know. I know. Poor guy ...

John: Poor guy? What do you mean? He doesn't sound very poor to me if he can afford a dozen ...

Lisa: No. I mean I feel sorry for him. He's in love with her—yes. But she's not in love with him.

John: How do you know? Did she say so?

Lisa: She doesn't even know who it is—and she says she doesn't really mind! She always ...

3. Listen to the following utterances: you will hear each one twice. Decide which of the questions, A or B, provides a suitable context for what you hear. The highlight is not transcribed here, so you must recognise which word is made prominent.

(1) They hired a car.

A. Did they take the car?

B. Did they hire bikes?

(2) No, the train was delayed.

A. Had she already arrived at the station?

B. Was the plane late?

(3) The bank's on the corner.

A. Where's the bank?

B. What's on the corner?

(4) I sent him a letter.

A. Aren't you going to send Tony a letter?

B. How does Mr Pringle know your news?

(5) It's next Tuesday.

A. Is it your birthday next week?

B. Was it your birthday last Tuesday?

Part 3 Post-Listening Activities

Listen to the conversation between Mother and the school principal in the film *Forrest Gump*.

Mother: Did you hear what I said, Forrest? You're the same as everybody else. You are no different.

Principal: Your boy is different, Mrs Gump. And his IQ is 75.

Mother: Well, we're all different, Mr Heincock.

Forrest: She wanted me to have the finest education, so she took me to the Greensboro County

Central School . . . I met the principal and all.

Principal: I want to show you something, Mrs Gump. Now this is normal. Forrest is right here. The state requires a minimum IQ of 80 to attend Public School, Mrs Gump. He's gonna have to go to a special school. And he'd be just fine.

Mother: What does normal mean anyway? He might be a bit on the slow side. But my boy Forrest is gonna get the same opportunities as everyone else. He's not going to some special school to learn how to repair tires. We're talking about 5 little points here. There must be somethin' can be done.

Unit 16

【Section 1】 Listen Accurately

Party games

Task 1 You will hear children describing four party games. Before you listen to the tape, discuss with your partner about how the things listed below are used in the games. Then listen to the tape and put them into the right places.

Words and expressions
thimble, bar of chocolate, jacket, pair of glove, scarf, dice, knife and fork, hat, bath cap, eggs, towel, roll of toilet paper

Game A	Game B	Game C	Game D

Task 2 Discussion: Think of a party game you know. Tell your partner about it.

(1) What do you need to play it?
(2) How many people do you need?
(3) What are the rules?
(4) How do you play it?
(5) How can you win?
(6) What is the punishment?

【Section 2】 Listen to Share

Friendship

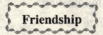

Task 1 Discuss with your partner about the following questions before listening to the tape.

(1) In your opinion, what does a good friend mean to people?
(2) What are some of the most important principles between good friends? In other words, what should good friends do and what shouldn't?

Task 2 Listen to the two conversations and answer these questions.

(1) What are the two friends talking about?
(2) Why is one friend worried?
(3) Do you think they are very good friends? Why?
(4) Why are the two friends arguing?
(5) Who got the job?
(6) Are they still angry with each other by the end of the conversation? How do you know?

Task 3 Discuss with your partner and decide the meaning of the following idioms in these two conversations. Then listen to the tape again and do the matching.

(1) give you the cold shoulder	A. communicate successfully
(2) be cut off from	B. believe easily
(3) be in the same boat	C. be cheated
(4) double-crossed	D. lose communication
(5) take you at your word	E. to humiliate
(6) get through to	F. stop fighting
(7) come between	G. have the same problem
(8) putting me down	H. cheated
(9) make up	I. hurt others' relationship
(10) be had	J. be unfriendly

【Section 3】 Listen to Acquire

Group discussion

Words and expressions

seminar, tutorial, originally, objective, interchangeably, arise from quote, interrupt, stimulating beneficial, exploit, break into formulate

Task 1 Listen for the gist—Questions for listening.

(1) What does the term "group discussion" mean?

(2) What are the two major aims of group discussion?

(3) Why is it hard for non-native speakers to take full advantage of group discussion?

Task 2 Listen for the details—True or False?

(1) The speaker has two main objectives in his talk.

(2) A tutorial was usually for twenty-five students.

(3) There are clear differences in purpose between seminars and tutorials.

(4) The most important aim of group discussions is to allow the tutor and his students to get to know each other.

(5) Group discussion can not be very helpful without students' active participation.

Task 3 Follow-up activity

Frequently a lecturer tries to help the listener follow easily what he is saying by showing the relationship between various statements he makes. The table below illustrates some of the ways in which this is achieved and the *connectives* commonly used.

+ relationship (= "and")			—relationship(= "but")
enumeration	addition	result	concession
Firstly Secondly Then Later Finally	Moreover Furthermore In addition Again	Therefore Thus	However Yet Nevertheless In spite of (this/that)

Now listen to the lecture again and, in the table below, give examples of the relationships listed by writing the connectives.

Relationship	Connective(s) used
enumeration	
Addition	
Result	
Concession	

【Section 4】 Listen Efficiently

Functions of intonation (2)

Part 1 Pre-listening Activities

Answer the following questions by reading the passage below.

(1) What is tone?

(2) How many kinds of tone are there in English? How about Chinese?

(3) Does tone convey meanings? What are they?

As they are speaking, speakers of English make the pitch of the voices rise and fall in a way that has meaning for their hearers. We call these pitch movements tones. There are two main kinds of tone in English: those which finally rise (↗ and \↗), and those which finally fall (↘ and /↘). Of these, the two which seen to occur most frequently are the \↗ and the ↘. Speakers use falling tones in parts of utterances that contain information they think is new for their hearers—when they are telling them something they don't already know. It may be information in response to a question, or it may be information the speakers present as new, something they want their hearers to know about or consider.

续表

Speakers use fall-rise tones in parts of utterances that contain ideas they think their hearers already know about or have experience of. They refer to something shared by themselves and the hearers at that point in the conversation. It may be something they both know about, or it may be something that has just been stated or implied in the conversation.

Part 2 Listening Task

1. Listen to this part of a conversation.

Dave: What shall we give Claire?

Gill: Well, as she likes reading, we could give her a book.

Listen again to what Dave says:

Dave: What shall we give Claire?

(1) Answer the following questions.

① Can you say in which direction the pitch of Cave's voice moves on 'give Claire'?

② Do you think they have just been talking about Claire?

③ Do you think they have already spoken about giving Claire something?

Now listen again to what Gill says:

Gill: Well, as she likes reading, we could give her a book.

(2) Answer the following questions.

① Can you say in which direction the pitch of Gill's voice moves on "reading" and on "book"?

② Does Gill assume that Dave knows Claire likes reading?

2. First listen to the whole of this conversation between Lisa and Tony, and then answer the following questions.

(1) ① What is Tony worrying about?

② Do you think that Lisa feels he really needs to be worried?

(2) Now, working with a partner, listen to the second part again.

① Try to identify any ↘ and \↗ tones which are not marked in the transcript below.

② Try to explain why Tony and Lisa have chosen to use a ↘ or a \↗ tone where you have marked them.

Tony: // ↘ I <u>MEAN</u> // I MANaged to answer all the QUESTions // and I THINK I said the right <u>THINGS</u> // ↘ but I <u>DON'T</u> think // I wore the right <u>CLOTHES</u> //

Lisa: // ↘ <u>WELL</u> // there's NO point in <u>WORRY</u>ing about it // what's <u>DONE</u> // is <u>DONE</u> //

Tony: // ↘ <u>YES</u> Lisa // ↘ I <u>KNOW</u> // there's NOTHING I can <u>DO</u> about it // ↘ of <u>COURSE</u> // I CAN'T <u>CHANGE</u> anything // but I CAN'T help <u>THINK</u>ing about it //

Now listen to the third part and do the same again.

Lisa: // ↘ I'm <u>SURE</u> // you needn't <u>WORRY</u> // what <u>DID</u> you wear // ↘ <u>ANY</u>WAY //

Tony: // I HAD to put my <u>JEANS</u> on //

Lisa: // Your <u>JEANS</u> // ↘ OH I <u>SEE</u> //

Tony: // But I wore a <u>TIE</u> //

Lisa: // \↗ NEVER <u>MIND</u> // you <u>SAID</u> the right things // \↗ <u>ANY</u>WAY //

3. Listen to the following utterances, which you will hear twice. In

each case mark the tones in the transcript and decide which of the questions, A or B, provide a suitable context for what you hear.

(1) I met ROBert // this MORNing //

A. Who did you meet today?

B. When did you meet Robert?

(2) He TOLD me // he was in LOVE //

A. What did he tell you?

B. How do you know he's in LOVE?

(3) She's started to WORRY // about her eXams //

A. How does Sue feel about her exams?

B. What is Sue worrying about?

(4) I learned SPANISH // at SCHOOL //

A. Where did you learn to speak Spanish?

B. Did you learn any languages at school?

4. Listen to the following utterances which you will hear twice. Decide which of the questions, A or B, provides a suitable context for what you hear.

(1) // When we've finished LUNCH // we'll look at the PHOTOS //

A. When can we see the Photos?

B. What shall we do after lunch?

(2) // Your use of intoNAtion // can change the MEANing //

A. What can change the meaning of what you say?

B. Why is intonation important?

(3) // The hoTEL // was very GOOD //

A. Did you enjoy your holiday?

B. What was the accommodation like?

(4) // You can GO // if you've FINished //

A. What shall we do now we've finished?

B. Can we go?

Part 3 Post-listening Activities

Listen the conversation between Forrest and his mother.

Forrest: What's the matter, momma?

Mother: I'm dying, Forrest. Come on in, sit down over here.

Forrest: Why are you dying, momma?

Mother: It's my time. It's just my time. Oh. Now, don't you be afraid, sweetheart. Death is just a part of life. Something we are all destined to do. I didn't know it, but I was destined to be your momma. I did the best I could.

Forrest: You did good, momma.

Mother: Well. I happen to believe you make your own destiny. You have to do the best with what God gave you.

Forrest: What's my destiny, momma?

Mother: You're gonna have to figure that our for yourself. Life is a box of chocolates, Forrest. You never know what you're gonna get.

Forrest: Momma always had a way of explaining things so I could understand them.

Mother: I will miss you, Forrest.

Forrest: She had got the cancer, and died on a Tuesday. I bought her a new hat with little flowers on it.

Unit 17

【Section 1】 Listen Accurately

What sort of shop are they in?

Task Listen to the dialogues and decide what sort of shops people are in. Fill in the chart.

	name of the shop	the clues that help you decide
(1)		
(2)		
(3)		
(4)		
(5)		
(6)		
(7)		
(8)		

【Section 2】 Listen to Share

The best way to learn English

Task 1 Discuss with your partner and list some of the good ways to learn English.

Task 2 Listen to a conversation and answer the questions.

(1) What method of learning English are the students discussing?

(2) Do they think it's a good way?

(3) What type of TV show does one speaker think is best for learning English?

(4) Why does one speaker know so much about television news?

Task 3 Listen to the conversation again and try to guess the meanings of these idioms in this conversation. Do the matching, please.

(1) make out	A. all of the details
(2) fills me in	B. explains only a little
(3) scratches the surface	C. understand the procedures
(4) got to the bottom of	D. is believable
(5) make sense of	E. explains to me
(6) read between the lines	F. found all the information

(7) the ins and outs G. became understandable

(8) know the ropes H. understand with little information

(9) downed on I. find a way to understand

(10) adds up J. recognize

【Section 3】 Listen to Acquire

Age and language learning

Task 1 Listen and choose one answer for each of the following questions.

(1) The main idea in this short talk was that ________.

A. teenagers are more difficult to teach than adults

B. Danish teenagers can learn Swedish faster than younger children can

C. adults are more logical than children are

D. the ability to learn languages increases with age

(2) This talk claimed that ________.

A. the ability to learn decreases with age

B. children are better language learners than adults

C. adults are able to learn more efficiently than children

D. teenagers learn less, in the same amount of time, than younger children

(3) Which of the following possible explanations for older students' superior achievement was not mentioned?

A. Adults know more about the world.

B. Adults can use logical thinking.

C. Adults have more self-discipline.

D. Adults can read better.

Task 2 Follow-up activity

(1) Tell your partner the age when you started learning English and talk about your ideas on English then.

(2) As a grown-up now, have you been benefited from the advantages mentioned above in your English study?

(3) Listen again and try to note down the key phrases the speaker used to express her ideas.

【Section 4】 Listen Efficiently

Functions of intonation (3)

Part 1 Pre-listening Activities

Study the roles and status of speakers.

In some conversations the relationship between the speakers means that one of them naturally takes a dominant role. Think, for example, of a manager speaking to a worker, a doctor to a patient or a teacher to a student. The ↗ tone is the appropriate referring tone for the dominant speaker to choose, but it would be inappropriate for the non-dominant speaker to use it. You will see that, by choosing the ↗ tone instead of the \↗ tone, speakers can exercise a sort of dominance in the conversation which may or may not be associated with their social status.

Part 2 Listening Task

In each of the following dialogues one of the speakers will take the dominant role. Decide which one and then, with a partner, practise reading the dialogues before listening to the recording. But remember that the recording presents only one of several possible ways of reading them.

1. Mrs Newell has gone to see the doctor and is discussing her problem with him.

   (N for Mrs Newell, D for Doctor)

   D: Where is the pain, Mrs Newell?

   N: Here, Doctor, in my chest.

   D: I see. Here?

   N: Yes, Doctor.

   D: Does it hurt when you cough?

   N: Yes, it does.

   D: How long have you had it?

   N: Six or seven weeks.

   D: Six or seven weeks? As long as that?

   N: I think so.

   D: Have you tried taking anything—for the cough, I mean?

   N: Well—the usual honey and hot lemon. And then I bought some cough syrup.

   D: Did it help?

   N: No, Doctor. That's why I've come to see you.

2. Jack Marsden has arranged to see his bank manager because he wants to borrow enough money to start buying a flat.

(J for Jack, B for his bank manager)

B: So, you're interested in some sort of loan, Mr Marsden?

J: That's right. You see, I want to raise enough money for a deposit on a small flat.

B: Do you mean to buy?

J: Yes. I don't want to go on renting.

B: I see. Do you think you can get a mortgage?

J: Yes. I've seen about that. You see, I've got a secure job with a good salary.

B: Is the flat for yourself? Will you be living there alone?

J: Yes. For the moment anyway. Why? Does that make any difference to the loan?

B: No, no. Just interested. That's all.

J: Do you need to know anything else? I've brought my contract with details of my salary.

B: Good. Yes, fine. And have you any securities? Shares in any companies? Insurance policies? Things like that?

Part 3 Post-listening Activities

1. Find a dialogue in a film you like best and practice it with your partner.
2. Each pair gives their performance to the class and let the class name the film.

Unit 18

【Section 1】 Listen Accurately

Handling an emergency

Task

A swimming instructor is demonstrating artificial respiration for two students. Put the pictures in the correct order by writing the number in the box in each picture. Then complete the sentences underneath the pictures.

Check for breathing. Listen at the ________ and ________

Make a tight seal over the ________. Give the first ________ as quickly as possible.

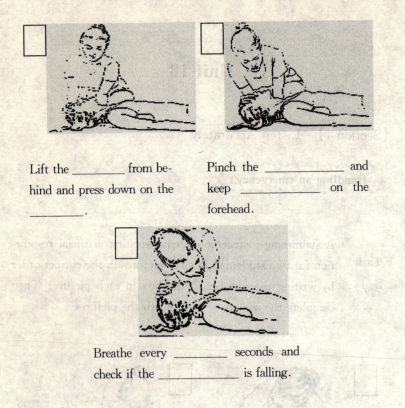

Lift the ________ from behind and press down on the ________.

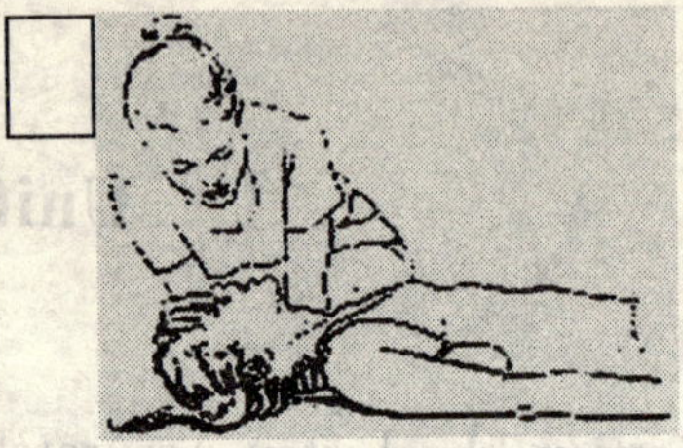

Pinch the ____________ and keep ____________ on the forehead.

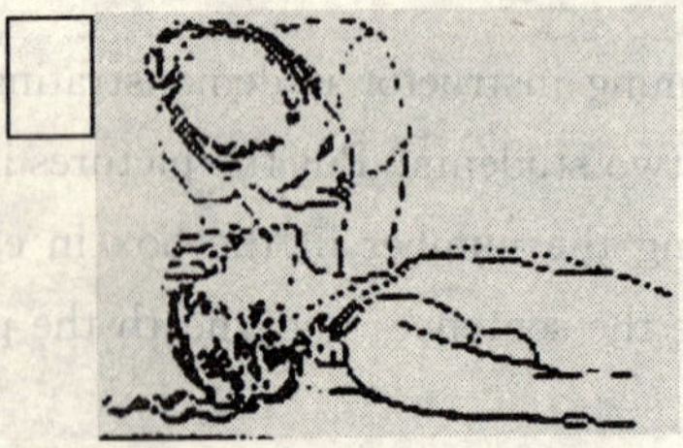

Breathe every ________ seconds and check if the ____________ is falling.

【Section 2】 Listen to Share

Marriage guidance council

David and Barbara Weiner have been married for nearly fifteen years. They have two children, Gary, aged eleven, and Debbie, who is nine. During the last couple of years David and Barbara haven't been very happy. They argue all the time. Barbara's sister advised them to go to a marriage counselor. A marriage counselor helps married couples to talk about their problems and to solve them, if possible. Sometimes they meet the counselor separately, and other times they are together for the session. This is David and Barbara's third session with Dr Joyce Sisters, the counselor.

Task 1 Pretend that you were Dr Joyce Sisters, the counselor. Try to take notes on both Barbara's and David's complain as you are listening to the tape.

Barbara	David

Task 2 How would you help them? What are your suggestions? Discuss with your partner, please.

【Section 3】 Listen to Acquire

Pronunciation achievement factors

Task 1 Listen and choose one answer for each of the following questions.

(1) The main idea in this talk was that ________.

A. it is impossible for foreign students to learn accurate pronunciation

B. females do not learn language better than males

C. the conclusions of Mr Suter's research are encouraging to language learners

D. if they know the factors helping pronunciation, students can achieve better results in learning pronunciation

(2) The four important factors related to the accuracy of pronunciation are ________.

A. personality, mother tongue, conversation with natives and natural ability

B. attitude about pronunciation, natural ability, conversation with natives and mother tongue

C. mother tongue, attitude about pronunciation, conversation with natives and natural ability

D. sex, attitude about pronunciation, conversation with natives and natural ability

(3) Which of the following is not true according to the results of the research by Mr Suter?

A. Out-going people learn pronunciation better than shy people.

B. It makes a difference if the student believes in the importance of pronunciation.

C. Natural ability is the least important factor in learning pronunciation.

D. If the student's own language is closer to English, the achievement is likely to be greater.

Task 2 Follow-up activity

(1) Has the report on the research brought good or bad news to you in your English study?

(2) Have you noted any relationship between your personality and your pronunciation?

(3) Are there any other factors you consider important to pronunciation achievement?

(4) Listen again and note down the key phrases used to express the major points in the report.

【Section 4】 Listen Efficiently

Thought group (1)

Part 1 Pre-listening Activities

1. Read the passage below.

You have been shown how speakers can use intonation to help listeners understand their messages. You may have noticed that in doing so, they divide speech into small "chunks." These chunks or thought groups are groups of words that go together to express one idea or thought. In written English, thought groups are marked by punctuation, for example, commas, full stops, capital letters and paragraphs. In spoken English, other ways are employed to help the listener understand messages. The most common signals are pauses and pitch change. These can be used like punctuation, to mark the introduction, continuation and conclusion of ideas in connected speech. An idea may involve only one thought group or several related thought groups.

2. Study the basic pattern of thought group markers.

(1) High pitch marks the beginning of a new idea.

(2) High pitch (often together with a short pause) marks the continuation of an idea.

(3) Low pitch and a pause mark the end of an idea.

Part 2 Listening Task

1. Listen to the following equations. Then practise saying them, using pauses and low pitch to show the end of each group.

   (1) $(A+B)\times C=Y$ (A plus B, multiplied by C, equals Y)

   (2) $A+(B\times C)=D$ (A, plus B multiplied by C, equals D)

   (3) $A-(B\times C)=Y$

   (4) $(A-B)\times C=Y$

   (5) $(X\div Y)-A=B$

2. Listen to the recorded mathematical calculations. Write down the answers. The correct answer depends on correct grouping.

3. Listen to the recorded excerpt of natural speech and write down

the two telephone numbers. Make sure you group the numbers together correctly.

Patrick's number: ①________

The radio station's number: ②________

4. It is important to group words together clearly so that the listener gets the right message. Listen and then practise saying this dialogue. Make sure you group the right couples together.

A: Who's coming tonight?

B: John.

A: Just John?

B: No, John and Susie.

A: No one else?

B: Well, there's Bob.

A: Alone?

B: No, with Anne.

A: So, that's John and Susie and Bob and Anne. Is that it?

B: Oh, and Gordon. On his own.

A: So that's John and Susie and Bob and Anne and Gordon.

B: Yes, that's right.

5. Two sentences written the same way have a different meaning. Marking the thought groups clearly helps distinguish the difference in meaning. Listen to the different emphasis in the following pairs of sentences. Which one do you hear, A or B ?

(1) A. The man and the woman dressed in black, came out of the restaurant.

B. The man, and the woman dressed in black, came out of the restaurant.

(2) A. Alfred said, "the boss is stupid."

B. "Alfred," said the boss, "is stupid."

(3) A. If you finish, quickly leave the room.

B. If you finish quickly, leave the room.

(4) A. Holding the handle firmly, turn the lever to the right.

B. Holding the handle, firmly turn the lever to the right.

(5) A. He sold his house, boat, and car.

B. He sold his houseboat, and car.

6. Throw away thought groups. Sometimes a speaker adds information or an idea that is not really essential, *ie* it can be "thrown away". We can signal that this thought group is less important than other ones by: a) lowering the pitch and b) saying it more quietly. Listen and underline the most important thought groups in A's sentences below, with your awareness of thrown away thought groups.

A: Alison is leaving work, so I've been told.

B: Really!

A: Don't tell anyone, but ... she's been sacked!

B: No!

A: Her husband, who's over there talking to Jean, is very upset about it.

B: Oh dear.

A: They're moving, so they say, to the south.

Part 3 Post-listening Activities

Discuss the following opinions to see whether you agree or disagree.

(1) Students need to be taught about thought group markers, because languages differ both in the way thought groups are marked and in the concept of what should be included in the

group.

(2) Many students usually do not notice pauses in their listening since they fail to realize that thought groups are as important as stress pattern of a word or sentence focus in spoken English.

(3) If there're no pauses in an utterance, native listeners may also have difficulty understanding a series of numbers, no matter how clearly each number is pronounced.

(4) Students can listen more efficiently by being reminded that words around each idea are often clearly grouped.

(5) The three basic signals that mark thought group boundaries are pause, pitch drop, and lengthening of final syllable.

Unit 19

【Section 1】 Listen Accurately

Apartment hunting

Task A man phones a building superintendent for information about an apartment for rent. Fill in the answers to his questions on the checklist.

Memo
Call about apt. in Gazette
Number of bedrooms:
Rent:
Includes
heat? *electricity?*
What floor:
Elevator?
Washers / dryers in bldg.?
Near shopping?
Quiet bldg.?
Address:
Who to see:
Time:
Other info:

【Section 2】 Listen to Share

Out of work

In the United States a lot of people are out of work. Tracy Kowalski is 19. She dropped out of high school two years ago and got a job as a check-out clerk in a supermarket. She was fired four months ago and hasn't been able to find another job yet. George Hartman is 54. Until last year he was a foreman at an automobile plant in Michigan. He had worked for the same company since he graduated from high school. He had a good job and a comfortable life. When the company cut back production last year, George was laid off.

Task Decide who produced the following statements and listen to the monologue to check with the tape.

(1) I'm on unemployment, but it isn't very much and I'm just fed up with standing in line to sign for it every other week.

(2) I've been turned down so many times that now I'm afraid of applying for a job.

(3) I'm really tired of going through the want ads.

(4) I'm interested in learning a new skill, but nobody wants to train me.

(5) I'm terrified of having nothing to do.

(6) There are at least fifty people for every job.

(7) I really don't want to leave my family and my friends.

(8) We have to be careful with expenses, and so I've given up

smoking.

(9) I'd take any job that came along.

(10) But she can't stand having me around the house all day.

(11) I'd enjoy having a job again—any job. It's not just the money.

(12) I guess I want to feel useful.

Tracy	George

Task 2 Discuss with your partner about the following questions.

(1) How does Tracy's father feel about her unemployment?

(2) Who gives Tracy some money now and then?

(3) What was Tracy interested in doing? Why?

(4) Why is it not easy for George to look for a job?

(5) How long had George worked?

(6) Why does George want to have a job?

【Section 3】 Listen to Acquire

Thought group markers

Task 1 Listen and choose one answer for each of the following questions.

(1) The main idea of this talk was that ________.

A. Each language has special way to mark thought groups

B. O' Malley knows the importance of thought group markers

C. It is very helpful for listeners to know thought group markers used by English speakers

D. Sometimes, English speakers pause at the end of their sentences

(2) The chief thought group marker in English is ________.

A. pronunciation

B. intonation

C. pauses

D. silence

(3) Which of the following is not true?

A. Written language substitutes punctuation for the spoken signals of intonation.

B. If algebra problems are spoken out loud, learners of English can hear the grouping.

C. The English listeners depends on the intonation signals in order to understand clearly.

D. If the thought groups are not clearly divided, the listener can get confused.

Task 2 Follow-up activity

(1) Summarize the functions and characteristics of though group markers.

(2) Have you noticed the signals in this lecture? Are they helpful to you?

(3) Listen again and note down the key phrases used for the ma-

jor points in the lecture.

【Section 4】 Listen Efficiently

Thought group (2)

Part 1 Pre-listening Activities

1. Read the excerpt from the speech by Dr Martin Luther King, August 28, 1963.

   "I have a dream that my four little children will one day live in a nation where they will not be judged by the colour of their skin, but by the content of their character . . . I have a dream that one day the state of Alabama . . . will be transformed into a situation where little black boys and black girls will be able to join hands with little white boys and white girls and walk together as sisters and brothers . . . "

2. Prepare the speech with your efforts to organize thoughts around your interpretation of the speech.
3. Practice the speech to each other in pairs.

4. Listen to the speech by Martin Luther King himself, paying attention to the different grouping you might have.

Part 2 Listening Task

1. Listen to the excerpts from a lecture on "Thought group markers". Then write down the text and mark the high and low pitch

and the pauses.

2. Listen to these phrases taken from the same lecture. Decide whether the end of each phrase is the end of an idea or not.

   Yes/No

   (1) ____________________

   (2) ____________________

   (3) ____________________

3. Listen to the phrases from a radio news bulletin about the death of Olof Palme, the Swedish Prime Minister. Listen to the introductory comment:

   "*The Swedish Prime Minister*, *Mr Olof Palme*, *has been assassinated*."

Did you notice the high pitch on "Swedish" to mark this new topic? Listen to the concluding remark about Olof Palme made by the English Prime Minister, Mrs Margaret Thatcher:

"... '*I shall miss Olof Palme very deeply*,' *she said*."

Did you notice the final very low pitch on "said" and then a long pause to mark the end of this topic? Listen to how the news reader introduces the next topic:

"*Now the other news* ..."

Did you notice the high pitch on "now"? Again, this marks a new topic. Listen again to the introductory and concluding remarks about Olof Palme and try and say them yourself at the same time.

4. Listen to these phrases taken from the same news bulletin about Olof Palme. Decide whether the end of each phrase is the end of an idea or not.

Yes/No

(1) ____________________

(2) ____________________

(3) ____________________

(4) ____________________

(5) ____________________

Now listen to the whole news bulletin. How many topics are there altogether?

Listen again to the last news item about Norway as a dictation.

Check your writing and then try and read it aloud using the same pauses and pitch changes as the news reader.

5. Listen to the conversation between Chris and his boss, Diana. When Diana pause, is she going to add something else, or has she finished what she wanted to say? If you think she will add something else, say "yes" after the "bleep". If you think she has finished, say "right". Example:

Diana: Oh, Chris, it's about the visitors ...

Chris: Yes?

Diana: They're coming on Thursday,

Chris: Right.

Now continue.

6. Listen to the excerpt from a conversation between a training manager from Telecom Headquarters (referred to here as THQ) and an interviewer.

(1) Mark the high pitch when each of the two speakers start speaking.

(2) Mark the long pause and the pitch when the first speaker finishes speaking.

"... and of course we're in constant touch with them by telephone yes tell me er some of the sorts of problems that you er get and that would call for a visit from THQ er well one of the problems would be where we discover that something has gone wrong ..."

7. Listen to four short excerpts from a different part of the same interview. In each case, decide if the speaker has said all he wants to say or not.

Yes/No

(1) ____________________

(2) ____________________

(3) ____________________

(4) ____________________

Part 3 Post-listening Activities

1. Make a report of current news on the radio.

2. Play the recording of current news and discuss it in class.

Unit 20

【Section 1】 Listen Accurately

Holiday plans

Task

A woman is discussing her holiday plans with a travel agent. Look carefully at the booking form. Listen to the conversation between the woman and the travel agent. Try to complete the booking form.

FREETIME HOLIDAYS BOOKING FORM		
Holiday Reference Number	Departure Date	Number of Nights
PASSENGERS NAME		
□ Mr □ Mrs □ Ms □ Miss	Initials	Surname
DESTINATION/TOUR		
□ HOTEL　　□ APARTMENT　　□ VILLA Name of the place:		

续表

ACCOMMODATION	Standard room	Superior room	Deluxe room	
Single				
Twin				
Triple				
MEAL PLAN	□ Room only	□ Room/breakfast	□ Half Board	□ Full Board
COST (Per person)				
SUPPLEMENTS	Accommodation	Meals	Departure date	Other
Total price				
DEPOSIT Enclosed please find deposit of ______	CREDIT CARDS Card No ______ I wish to pay by credit card. Signature ______			

【Section 2】 Listen to Share

The driving test

Task 1 Before you listen to the tape, discuss the following questions in groups.

(1) What does the driving test consist of in China?

(2) Is there a written test?

(3) What maneuvers do you have to carry out in the test?

(4) Do people often pass the test when they take it for the first time?

Task 2 Now you will hear a conversation between Jill, who has just taken her driving test, and her husband Bob. Jill failed the test. As you listen, put the events in the correct order.

A. I didn't look right before pulling out into the main road.
B. The examiner calmly filled in his form.
C. When I had to park, I got too close to another parked car and scraped it.
D. Forgot to take the handbrake off.
E. I was asked to read a number plate about thirty yards away.
F. The examiner slammed the brakes on and put his hand to his forehead.
G. I made a cyclist swerve.
H. I was shaking like a leaf.
I. People behind me started hooting.
J. When I did the emergency stop, I skidded.

(1) ______ (2) ______ (3) ______ (4) ______
(5) ______ (6) ______ (7) ______ (8) ______
(9) ______ (10) ______

【Section 3】 Listen to Acquire

Techniques for oral presentation

Task 1 Listen and choose one answer for each of the following questions.

(1) Which of the following has best summarized the talk?

A. There is big difference between spoken and written English.

B. Tips for successful oral presentations.

C. Suggestions for better listening.

D. It is important to give enough time for the listeners to think both before and after each new idea.

(2) The speakers can help listeners by ______.

A. pausing, paraphrasing and using filler words

B. using filler words, speaking slowly and paraphrasing

C. speaking more slowly and providing enough thinking time for listeners

D. packing new information rapidly but delivering slowly

(3) What are the filler words?

A. The words contain no message but give listeners time to think.

B. The words have a lot of information.

C. The words are made of failed ones.

D. The words do help listeners to think.

Task 2 Follow-up activity

(1) Have you ever given a speech in public? Did you have your audience in mind while you were speaking? What did you do to make yourself understood?

(2) Pick up some of the filler words used in this lecture. Can you tell the difference between the filler words and key words in the lecture?

(3) Listen again and note down the key phrases used for the ma-

jor points in the lecture.

【Section 4】 Listen Efficiently

Listening for positive results

Part 1 Pre-listening Activities

1. Read and sum up the ideas in the following passage.

A noticeable feature of listening in a foreign language is that if you are not proficient in this language, you will be diminished in intelligence. Your processing capacity is so taken up with your struggle for the meaning of the spoken language that you can hardly remember the purpose of your listening. Therefore, we have to be reminded of the listening activities carried on in our own language. The listening skills we actually employ, without our consciousness, in our own language need to be transferred into doing that in a foreign language with great consciousness. The success in the transference will lead to the success in listening to a foreign language.

2. Discuss the ideas in pairs with your commentary

Part 2 Listening Task

1. Listen to the first part of the talk and answer the following questions.
   (1) What is the difference between listening and hearing?
   (2) What can a listener do in receiving the message?
   (3) What are the purposes of listening in real life?

(4) How many kinds of listening are mentioned in the talk? What are they?

2. Listen to the second part of the talk and fill in the blanks.

Suggestions for achievements in intensive listening

(1) Try to ______________________________________.

(2) Attempt to __________________________________.

(3) Watch ______________________________________.

(4) Provide _____________________________________.

(5) Try to ______________________________________.

3. Listen to the last part of the talk and answer the following questions.

(1) What is casual listening?

(2) Do you have any casual listening, in English or in Chinese, everyday?

(3) What do you usually listen to?

4. Listen to the complete talk and discuss the following questions in pairs.

(1) What is the difference in listening to English and listening to our own language?

(2) Are all the suggestions suitable for our own daily practice in listening ?

(3) Make a list of suggestions for our listening in English.

5. Now listen to a piece of news and answer the following questions.

(1) What is this piece of news about?

(2) In which part of the world did that happen?

(3) Do you have some ideas about this country?

Part 3 Post-Listening Activities

Watch a film and enjoy it.

Transcript

Unit 1

【Section 1】

Numbers: numeral system

Task

(1) 466	(2) 572	(3) 761	(4) 829	(5) 653
(6) 275	(7) 187	(8) 593	(9) 960	(10) 640
(11) 360	(12) 330	(13) 316	(14) 814	(15) 218
(16) 113	(17) 302	(18) 408	(19) 601	(20) 804
(21) 203	(22) 503	(23) 106	(24) 409	(25) 457
(26) 321	(27) 515	(28) 392	(29) 519	(30) 919
(31) 698	(32) 481	(33) 728	(34) 777	(35) 820
(36) 104	(37) 419	(38) 886	(39) 559	(40) 632

【Section 2】

A story: A difficult woman

My mother always said that my grandmother was a very difficult woman but we, her grandchildren, loved her very much because she was always happy. My mother went to see her every month and my brother and I went with her. We always slept at grandmother's house for one night when we went to visit her because she lived three hundred kilometres from our town.

One Friday my grandmother telephoned when my mother was out shopping so my brother spoke to her. "The leg's broken! The leg's broken!" said my grandmother. I went to the shops to find my mother and tell her the bad news. We ran home quickly. My mother telephoned my grandmother but she didn't answer so my mother telephoned the police station near grandmother's house. We were very worried. About an hour later the police telephoned my mother and said, "It's OK. Your mother's fine."

"But what about her broken leg?" my mother asked.

"Oh," said the policeman. "She hasn't got a broken leg. The leg of her favourite chair broke." My brother and I thought this was very funny but my mother didn't. We heard my mother tell the policeman, "She's a very difficult woman!"

【Section 3】

The geography of the United States (1)

The United States covers 3,600,000 square miles. Within this area are fifty states. Two of the states, Alaska and Hawaii, are separated from the other forty-eight states. The Gulf of Mexico and three oceans, the Atlantic, the Pacific, and the Arctic, lie along the sides of the country. Also, two countries border the US. Mexico is to the southwest, and Canada is to the north. The United States has two major mountain ranges, the Appalachian Mountains in the east and the Rocky Mountains in the west. Three large rivers flow in the area between the Rockies and the Appalachians. They are the Ohio, the Missouri, and the Mississippi.

【Section 4】

Listening and understanding

A student learning English often finds the following three problems when he listens to talks or lectures.

Firstly, he doesn't always identify all the words correctly. I refer here to known words, *ie* words which the student would recognize in print. Let's examine some of the reasons for this particular difficulty. In writing, there are spaces between each words. In speech, however, it's very difficult to decide where one word finishes and the next one begins. In writing, all the letters are easy to identify. In speech, many of the sounds cause a student difficulty and he fails to identify them. Some words in English have a weak form which non-native speakers only identify with difficulty. The students also sometimes find it difficult to hear the unstressed syllable in a word. This problem doesn't occur in print.

The second main problem is the difficulty of remembering what's been said. Words in print are permanently fixed in space. They can, therefore, be studied again and again. In speech, however, words disappear immediately after they've been spoken. The listener has to concentrate very hard, therefore, on identifying and understanding them immediately. There is no chance of hearing them a second time.

Thirdly, there's the problem of following the argument. Students may frequently have difficulty with this even when they understand and remember all the words. I want to suggest three reasons for this. Firstly, the students don't always recognize the important points. Secondly, in trying to understand small points, they may miss the big ones. Thirdly, because they're concentrating on taking notes, they may miss developments in the argument.

In addition, students have difficulty understanding different accents. Many lectures will have a BBC-type accent, though others will have a different pronunciation. It's usually the vowels which are pronounced differently, but sometimes the consonants, too. The style of English a lecturer uses may also cause problems. A more formal style can generally be followed more easily than a colloquial one.

All these factors combine to make it a formidable task for students to follow lectures comfortably. It's clearly helpful to be aware of the problems and to get as much practice as possible in listening to and trying to understand spoken English.

Unit 2

【Section 1】

Numbers: hundreds, thousands

Task 1

(1) 5,896	(2) 7,906	(3) 4,494	(4) 5,515
(5) 26,960	(6) 75,682	(7) 28,657	(8) 38,024
(9) 57,490	(10) 63,818	(11) 99,233	(12) 16,997

(13) 621,844 (14) 392,835 (15) 302,798
(16) 275,390 (17) 879,930 (18) 911,909
(19) 719,056 (20) 104,308
(21) 6,752,431 (22) 9,879,041 (23) 8,100,003
(24) 5,663,174 (25) 3,312,765 (26) 2,007,009
(27) 4,276,390 (28) 1,060,030 (29) 12,456,800
(30) 50,060,120 (31) 44,731,556 (32) 68,238,730
(33) 140,732,55 (34) 164,504,832 (35) 193,116,583
(36) 150,040,070 (37) 647,325,360 (38) 730,004,015
(39) 343,506,104 (40) 975,075,055

Task 2

Cookies are a big business in the US. One shop in Boston sells 30,000 warm cookies every day, mostly chocolate chip. On the West Coast, a 45-year-old American, Wally Amos, has made his fortune from chocolate chip cookies.

When Amos was 13 years old, he went to live with his Aunt Delia, who made cookies for him, from a recipe created in 1929. Amos joined the Air Force in 1953, and his aunt sent him cookies so he wouldn't be homesick. For Amos, as for most Americans, cookies represent love and home.

After the Air Force, Amos worked for other people for 14 years. In 1975, he decided he could make more money if he had his own business. He talked some friends into investing $ 24,500 in a cookie business. He worked 18 hours a day, baking cookies and thinking of clever ways to promote them. For instance, he traded $ 750 worth of cookies for advertising time on a local radio station. In 1976, he began selling cookies in 15 department stores on the East Coast. That year the cookie corporation took in $ 300,000. By

1982 the company made $7,000,000. Amos now has 150 employees, and they produce more than 7,000 pounds of cookies a day.

【Section 2】

A story: meeting famous people

I always wanted to meet a famous person and I met one last summer by accident. I decided to have a weekend in London and visit some old friends from university who worked at the Savoy hotel. I couldn't stay at the Savoy because it was very expensive so I found a cheap place to stay.

The first night I was there we all went out to a club. We didn't stop dancing until three o'clock. I had to wait an hour to get a taxi back to my hotel. When the taxi stopped, a man ran in front of me and opened the taxi door. I usually hate to be angry with people but I was cold, tired and I wanted to go to bed.

"I waited for an hour for this taxi," I said. "You can't have it!"

"I must have it," the man said. "My wife is having a baby. I promise to pay for the taxi driver to come back and take you where you want to go. Give the driver the address now and I'll give you the money. Please!"

"Yes, of course," I said.

I waited but the taxi didn't come back. However, I got another one quite quickly.

The next day I saw in the newspaper a picture of the man who took my taxi. the headline said "FAMOUS FILM DIRECTOR'S

WIFE HAS BABY IN TAXI."

The next day I showed my friends the newspaper. "That was my taxi," I said.

【Seciton 3】

The geography of the United States (2)

The US is a too large and varied country to sum up in short explanation. To understand some of its differences, it can be divided into six regions: the Northeast, the Central Basin, the Southeast, the Great Plains, the Mountains and Deserts and the Coast Valleys. Besides there are Alaska and Hawaii, the forty-ninth and fiftieth state.

Look at the Northeast section of the map where New York is the largest city. Now it is the financial center of the United States. The gentle sloping prairie land of the Central Basin was once the frontier to those who crossed the Appalachian Mountains. There the States of Ohio, Indiana, Illinois, Iowa and Nebraska are known as the Corn Belt. Now look back across the Appalachian Mountains, south from Washington, DC, into the Southeast. In the State of Virginia, Richmond was the capital of the Southern Confederacy during the Civil War, and Monticello was the home of Thomas Jefferson, principal writer of the Declaration of Independence and third President of the US.

The Great Plains is a hard country. The heat of the summer is scorching, the winter is freezing. The wind blows fiercely. Its scarcity drove the settlers on across the plains as far as they could go. Only the Red Indians knew how to survive here. The Rocky Mountains lie in the Mountains and Deserts region. They are the long back-bone of the continent—over 4, 200 meters high and 560 kilometres wide in Utah and Colorado. Somewhere near Los Angeles, stretching northward along the Pacific Coast, is the fertile region called the Coast Valleys. All the three Pacific coast States—Washington, California and Oregon—face toward the Orient. Cargoes of fish, timber and fruit are shipped from the ports of San Francisco, Portland and Seattle to Asia.

Seattle is the gateway to Alaska, which is so far north. Fishing, mining, lumber and oil make Alaska rich in natural resources. Hawaii is a string of sun-drenched islands over 3, 200 kilometres out in the Pacific Ocean from the coast of California.

Alaska and Hawaii and all six regions of the US are in sharp contrast to each other. The geography and climate and kinds of people who have settled there have shaped their destinies differently. But all are bound together by a way of life that is American.

【Section 4】

The sound of English natural speed

Part 2

2. (1) Laughter has no foreign accent.
   (2) Work well done is art.
   (3) To teach is to learn again.
   (4) Try to put it off for another hour.
   (5) Talk it over with the other operator.

(6) The accounts have all been updated.

(7) Send them a FAX about the problem

(8) Don't even think about it!

3. (R for Rose, J for Jack)

R: I love you, Jack.

J: Don't you do that. Don't you say your good byes. Not yet, do you understand me?

R: I'm so cold.

J: Listen Rose, you're gonna get out of here. You're gonna go on and you're gonna make lots of babies, and you're gonna watch them grow. You're gonna die and old, an old lady warm in her bed. Not here. Not this night, not like this, do you understand me?

R: I can't feel my body.

J: Winning that ticket, Rose, was the best thing that ever happened to me. It brought me to you. And I'm thankful for that, Rose, I'm thankful. You must, you must do me this honor. You must promise me that you'll survive, that you won't give up. No matter what happens, no matter how hopeless, promise me now, Rose, and never let go of that, promise.

R: I promise.

J: Never let go.

R: I'll never let go, Jack. I'll never let go.

Unit 3

【Section 1】

Names, addresses and telephone numbers

Task 1

(1) My name's Jameson. That's J-A-M-E-S-O-N. I'll spell it again for you. J-A-M-E-S-O-N.

(2) Do you need my full name? My first name's Juliet. J-U-L-I-E-T. Yes, J-U-L-I-E-T. And my surname's Henderson. Hen-der-son-H-E-N-D-E-R-S-O-N.

(3) A: My Christian name is Stephen.

B: Now, there are different ways of spelling that, aren't there?

A: Yes. Mine's P-H.

B: Pardon?

A: You spell it S-T-E-P-H-E-N.

B: Thank you.

(4) A: Place of birth, please madam.

B: Loughborough. L-O-U-G-H-B-O-R-O-U-G-H. Would you like me to spell it again? L-O-U-G-H-B-O-R-O-U-G-H.

(5) Hello, I'd like to order a book by Gerald Leary. Hello? It's not a very good line, is it? Gerald Leary. Gerald-G-E-R-A-L-

D. Leary-L-E-A-R-Y. That's it. The title of the book is *The Secret Life of Plants*.

(6) Hello, er-I have a reservation. The name's Mahoney-M-A-H-O-N-E-Y.

(7) My surname's Bailey-B-A-I-L-E-Y.

(8) A: Where do you live?

B: A suburb of London called Greenwich.

A: G-R-E-N-

B: No, no. G-R-double E-N-W-I-C-H. Greenwich.

(9) A: Hello. I have an appointment with Miss Jenkins.

B: Your name please?

A: Seabourne. S-E-A-B-O-U-R-N-E.

(10) A: I'm living in a place called Gloucester.

B: How do you spell that?

A: G-L-O-U-C-E-S-T-E-R. Gloucester.

Task 2

(1) (649)545-4867 (2) (8610)6647-8219

(3) (141)6945-1816 (4) (612)4546-8016

(5) (309)822-5920 (6) (670)266-3315

Task 3

(1) A: Well, look, we must keep in touch. Let me give you my address.

B: Right. OK.

A: John Mitchell

B: John Mitchell. Is that two "l"s?

A: Yes. M-i-t-c-h-e- double l.

B: Right.

A: And the address is 15—

B: 15.

A: Brougham Place.

B: Br—How do you spell Brougham?

A: B-r-o-u-g-h-a-m. Brougham.

B: Oh. Ridiculous.

A: And that's Oxford.

B: Right.

A: Oh, I'll give you my telephone number.

B: Telephone number. Yeah.

A: 223.

B: 223.

A: 6790.

B: 6790. Right, right. I'll give you a ring.

(2) A: Look, I've got a friend in Singapore. You could call on him if you've got time. Do you want his address?

B: Yes, I'd love it. Thank you.

A: Well, his name is Joe Harding. J-o-e. Harding, H-a-r-d-i-n-g. And the address is The Manhattan Building.

B: Manhattan.

A: Manhattan.

B: The Manhattan Building.

A: 2563 Orchard Road.

B: That was 2563.

A: Yes, that's right.

B: Orchard Road.

A: Singapore.

B: Singapore.

A: And the telephone number is 236 47539.

B: I've got it.

【Section 2】

Hotel check-in

(R for Receptionist, G for Guest)

R: Can I help you, sir?

G: Hello, I'd like a room for the night.

R: Do you have a reservation?

G: No, I don't.

R: OK. Just the one night?

G: Yes.

R: And one person?

G: One person, yes.

R: Would you like an Executive at $125 or a Standard at $95?

G: Just a Standard.

R: OK... Do you have a preference for a twin or a double-bedded room?

G: Twin, please.

R: Do you have a preference for smoking or non-smoking?

G: Non-smoking, please.

R: OK. You're in room 760.

G: OK.

R: How will you be settling your account, sir?

G: Visa.

R: By Visa card. May I take an imprint of your Visa card?

G: Here you are.

R: Thank you. And the name, sir, is...?

G: Paul Smith.

R: And may I take your home address, please?

G: It's 5383 Collins Avenue, Miami.

R: And do you have a zip code?

G: 23892.

R: OK, sir. Because you're not a British citizen, I'll require your passport in order to complete the registration.

G: Here it is.

R: Thank you very much.

G: Does the rate include breakfast?

R: No, it doesn't. Breakfast is $7.50 for continental and $9.95 for English and is served in the Brasserie Restaurant on this floor from 6:30 all morning, or you can order in your room through room service at no extra charge.

G: OK.

R: This is your registration card. Can you just check through the details, please?

G: Yes. And sign here.

R: OK.

G: Thank you. Here's your credit card, passport, and here's your key. It's room 760 on the seventh floor. The elevator is on the right. If you just tell a porter your room number, he'll follow you up with the luggage.

R: Thank you very much.

G: Enjoy your stay.

【Section 3】

Schools in the United States

There are four kinds of schools in the United States. They are elementary school, junior high school, senior high school, and college. Elementary school is from kindergarten through sixth grade. Junior high school is from seventh grade through ninth grade. Senior high school is from tenth grade through twelfth grade. After senior high school, students study in college.

High school students study in class about five hours every day. In addition, some students join clubs such as a drama club, a foreign language club, or a photography club. Other students participate in sports such as basketball, football, baseball, and track.

College students study very hard. They attend classes about fifteen hours every week. In addition, they study a lot after class. They have to read their textbooks, write papers, and study for their tests. Many students study by themselves from three to five hours every day.

【Section 4】

Some characteristics of spoken English

Part 2

1. Every sound of every language is within every language. So, what happens with adults? People learn their native language and stop listening for the sounds they never hear; then they lose the

ability to hear those sounds. Later, when you study a foreign language, you learn a lot of spelling rules that take you still further away from the real sound of that language—in this case, English. The trouble after you know a great deal of English is that you know a great deal about English: You have a lot of preconceptions and, unfortunately, misconceptions about the sound of English. What we are going to do here is to teach you to hear again.

2. You may have notice that I talk fast and often run my words together. Native speakers may often tell people who are learning English to "slow down" and to speak clearly". This is meant with the best intentions, but it is exactly the opposite of what a student really needs to do. If you speak fairly quickly and with strong intonation, you will be understood more easily.

   By seeing and hearing simultaneously, you'll learn to reconcile the differences between the appearance of English (spelling) and the sound of English (pronunciation and the other aspects of accent).

   Just like your own language, conversational English has a very smooth, fluid sound. If you speak word by word, you'll end up sounding mechanical and foreign.

   Connect words to form sound group. Instead of thinking of each word as a unit, think of sound units, which make a sentence flow smoothly, like peanut butter—never really ending and never really starting, just flowing along.

3. Accent is a combination of three main components: intonation (speech music), liaisons (word connections) and pronunciation (the spoken sounds of vowels, consonants, and combinations).

Part of the difference is that grammar and vocabulary are systematic and structural—the letter of the language. Accent is free form, intuitive and creative—the spirit of the language.

You can use your accent to say what you mean and how you mean it.

Word stress conveys meaning through tone or feeling, which can be much more important than the actual words that you use.

Part 3

2. (1) When I was about 13 they said, "you're going to have a brace", and I thought "Oh yeah, you know, a simple little band round my teeth", and they, they showed me this picture and I had to have it top and bottom, and every tooth was ringed round with metal and a metal tab put on the front, and then a wire linking all the teeth together. I don't think that they need to do that, because my teeth, stuck out like that, because I sucked that finger, and all I had was a metal band, one thin band across. But mine were sort of like a zig-zag along the bottom. And a real mess, weren't they? Ah, I see. And the eye teeth were, yeah, I had hoops on my eye teeth. Sort of, they're very good now, aren't they? Ninety degrees, ninety degrees round. Oh, I see. And then I had elastic bands linking my top teeth to the bottom teeth. Oh my God. Because my jaws were in the wrong order; and I had this on from thirteen.... they said it was going to be on for a year and it was on for three and a half; and I didn't speak for about... because I wasn't supposed to eat between meals, and I hardly spoke for about three years because it was such an effort with these elastic bands which used to pin my mouth back.

Unit 4

【Section 1】

Times and dates

Task 1

(1) You are listening to x98.5 on your FM dial—the jazz station. The time now is just a minute away from two o'clock.

(2) This is the BBC. The time is six fifteen.

(3) This is 1010 News Radio. The station with all the news, all the time. Time now is 9:30.

(4) This is your station for easy listening, KABC. The time right now is going on 5:05.

(5) Thank you for calling Cinema World. Today in Cinema A we are showing *Dances with Wolves* starring Kavin Costner. Show times are 3:40, 5:05, 7:55, and 11:00.

(6) In Cinema B we are showing *Pretty Woman*. Show times are 4:30, 6:45, 8:30, and 10:45.

Task 2

(1) This is Dr Costello's office. We're calling to change your dental appointment to August 3rd at 9:30 in the morning. Thank you.

(2) Hi, Don. It's Sue. I'm calling about Cindy's birthday party. It's on July 28th at 8 pm. Are you free? I'll call you lat-

er.

(3) Hello, Don. This is Aunt Betty. How are you, darling? Listen, I'm coming to town next month. I'd love to see you. I'm arriving on August the tenth at 11:15 in the morning. I'll call you from the airport. Bye!

(4) Hi, Don. This is Ted. Listen, we can't play tennis on Saturday. Are you free Sunday afternoon, July 26th, around three?

(5) Hello, Don. This is Francis. I'll be back from my trip on Tuesday, September 22nd. Let's meet in my office that Tuesday around 6 pm, OK? Let me know.

(6) This is Star Travel. We've booked your flight to New Orleans for next month. You leave on August 2nd on flight 101 from Kennedy Airport at 2 pm.

【Section 2】

A story from Vietnam

The taxi driver finished work about nine o'clock in the evening. He was tired and hot and he wanted to get home quickly. On his way home it started to rain heavily. He saw a young girl under a tree near the road. The next village was four kilometres away.

"Perhaps she wants a lift in my taxi," he thought. He stopped the taxi and asked the young girl, "Do you want a lift home?"

"Thank you," she said, "but I haven't got any money."

"That's OK. I don't want any money from you," said the taxi driver.

"I live in the house on the hill," said the girl.

The girl got into the taxi and the taxi driver drove her home.

He went to the house and knocked on the door.

An old woman came to the door.

"I drove your daughter home—here she is."

"What?" asked the old woman angrily. "My daughter died five years ago under a tree."

She went back into the house and closed the door in the taxi driver's face.

The taxi driver turned round to ask the girl some questions, but she wasn't there. He never saw her again.

【Section 3】

Higher education in the United States

Higher education is education above the high school level. Community colleges, colleges and universities, and graduate programs at universities give students higher education. Community colleges have two-year programs. Many students at community colleges study subjects such as automobile repair, electricity, and photography. Both universities and colleges have four-year programs. Students study subjects such as history, literature, engineering, computer science, and business. Universities also have graduate programs for students who want to do advanced study after they finish four-year programs.

A university has undergraduate students and graduate students. Students are undergraduate students until they finish four years of study. After four years, they can become graduate students. Undergraduate students must take many different courses in addition to the courses in their majors, and they earn bachelor's degrees when they graduate. Graduate students usually study only courses in their majors. Some graduate students study only one or two years and earn master's degrees. Other graduate students study a longer time and earn doctor's degrees.

【Section 4】

Linking (1)

1. (1) I think, first of all, we ought, to ask him.

   (2) Is he busy on Monday evening?

2. **Conversation 1**

   A: We were riding down First near James, heading toward the water. A car came from around the corner. I guess he didn't see us or may be he was a little drunk. Who knows! Anyway, he sped directly past us, missing our bikes by less than an inch.

   B: Was any one else around?

   A: No. And what's more, he never even looked back. Probably didn't even know he'd run a stop sign.

   B: Wonder if he hurt anyone else?

   A: It wouldn't surprise me a bit.

   Conversation 2

   A: What was that all about? I've never seen Bob so edgy. Did something happen?

B: Not that I know of. But I just happened to mention taking a day off and he about hit the roof. It's not the first time it's happened this week, either.

A: That doesn't sound like him at all. Maybe he's under some pressure.

B: Possibly. I just wish he wouldn't take it out on me.

Unit 5

【Section 1】

Money system

Task 1

2 nickels
3 dimes
2 pennies and 2 quarters
3 dimes and 1 quarter
1 dime, 2 nickels and 1 quarter

Task 2

(1) Let's see. Soup. That's two for a dollar. Tomatoes—$2.50. A bottle of shampoo—$6.50. So that comes to $10.00 and your change is $10.00.

(2) OK. Now let me see what you've got. The CD is $14.95, and the cassette—oh, a good one—my favorite group—it's

on sale for $4.95. So, let me see—that comes to $19.90, so here's your change, ten cents.

(3) Yes, can I help you? OK. Let's see. The newspapers are $1.50, and the magazines will cost another... $8.15. Yes, so that's, let me see, $9.65, right? Here's your change, $7.35.

(4) So you're taking the T-shirt—nice choice. The color suits you. OK, that's $4.95, then the socks. They're another $3.20, so that's $8.15, and here's your change, $11.52.

(5) Hmm, I like chocolates too. OK, that's $9.50 for the chocolates. And chocolate chip cookies, too. Mm. You really do like chocolates. The cookies are $2.99. So that's $12.49. And here's your change, $5.51.

(6) Is this all? OK. Let's see. Now the magazines are $6.25. And you're taking the book? That's $12.00. So that comes to $18.25 altogether. And here's your change. That's a dollar seventy-five.

【Section 2】

A story: Sunset Boulevard

At the beginning of the film a young scriptwriter, Joe Gillis, is driving through Los Angeles. He has no work and no money, and he can't pay for his new car. Some people are looking for him because they want to take his car back so he hides it in the garage of a big house on Sunset Boulevard. The house belongs to an old film star called Norma Desmond. She lives there with a butler who was once her husband and who also directed her films. She lives with her memories of the time when she was famous, watching her old films and reading letters which she believes are from her fans, but which her butler writes. She wants to return to the screen and become famous again so when she meets Joe she asks him to write a filmscript for her. She also wants him to live at her house while he is writing it.

Joe doesn't want to live like a prisoner in this strange house, but he is happy to have a job and to take money and expensive clothes from Norma.

Soon there are problems. Norma falls in live with Joe. Also, the man who she wants to direct her new film, Cecil B. de Mille, does not like the filmscript.

Then Joe falls in love with a young writer and tries to leave Norma. She shoots him saying, "No one ever leaves Norma Desmond."

In the most famous scene at the end of the film the police come to take her away. The photographers and journalists are waiting as she walks down the stairs, and her last words are "All right, Mr de Mille. I'm ready for my close-up".

【Section 3】

The Declaration of Independence

1776 or the Fourth of July will immediately remind an American of the Declaration of Independence, the fundamental document establishing the United States as a nation. The Declaration was ordered and approved by the Continental Congress, and written largely by Thomas Jefferson. It declared the independence of the 13 original colonies from Great Britain, offered reasons for the separation, and laid out the principles for which the Revolutionary War was fought.

In 1787 the Constitution of the United States was drafted in Philadelphia. It was ratified in 1788, and put into practice in 1789. It is the oldest written constitution in the world—durable because it is a general document that can be interpreted for changing times. Or it can be amended. This has been done just 26 times.

The District of Columbia, sandwiched between the States of Maryland and Virginia, was set aside in the 1790's as the site for the new nation's capital. It was named Washington after the first President.

【Section 4】

Part 1

The Greatest Love of All

I believe the children are our future,
Teach them well and let them lead the way.
Show them all the beauty they possess inside,
Give them a sense of pride
  to make it easier.
Let the children's laughter remind us how we used to be.
Everybody's searching for a hero,
People need someone to look up to.

I never found anyone who fulfilled my needs,
A lonely place to be
  until I learned to depend on me.

I decided long ago
  never to walk in anyone's shadow.
If I fail, if I succeed,
At least I live as I believe
No matter what they take away from me,
  they can't take away my dignity,
  because the greatest love of all is happening to me.

I found the greatest love of all inside of me,
The greatest love of all is easy to achieve,
Learning to love yourself,
It is the greatest love of all.

Linking (2)

Part 2

1. (2) A: How often do I have to do it?
   B: You ought to do every exercise once a week.
   A: Do I have to do every exercise?
   B: Yes, it should take you about two hours. Though I don't suppose it will.

   (4) A: Actually, I ought to practise more regularly I suppose.
   B: Well, don't worry about it. I often forget myself.
   A: Perhaps we ought to try and go together.

   (5) A: How's it going, Edward?
   B: Not bad at all. It's not exactly a busy place though.
   A: Where are you staying?
   B: Just a little pub on the edge of town.

A: And what are you doing on your own?

B: Not a lot actually. This evening there's a match on TV, so I'll get a snack in town and watch a bit of football afterwards.

2. (2) A: Can I help you, sir?

B: Yes, I'm in a rush I'm afraid. Can I have a piece of apple cake please, with ice cream?

A: Certainly, sir. I'll ask the waiter to come over as soon as possible.

(4) A: Switch off the light, David. It's almost eleven.

B: I'm scared of the dark. I think I heard a noise. Look over there! Something on the window ledge is moving.

Unit 6

【Section 1】

Forecasting the weather

A weatherman gives the forecast on the TV evening news. Write the predicted weather conditions for the weekend on the map next to the name of the city.

(A for Anchorwoman, W for Weatherman)

A: ...and that's the Friday night news. Now over to Dave Spellman for the weekend weather forecast. Dave, what do you have in store for us this weekend?

W: Well, Linda, it's still raining here in Chicago, and it looks like that rain is going to continue through the weekend. It'll be cloudy tomorrow with scattered showers, and the outlook for Sunday—more rain and colder. The predicted high for tomorrow is forty-five degrees Fahrenheit, but the thermometer is expected to dip to the freezing point tomorrow night, with a temperature of thirty-two degrees. I'm afraid colder weather is on its way!

Let's take a look now at the weather across the country. Showers expected tomorrow down the West Coast as far south as San Francisco. Fair weather in the low seventies predicted for the Los Angeles area; fair in San Diego.

There's a cold front from Canada moving down through the western states. Thirty-eight degrees in Denver, Colorado, with thirty-mile-an-hour winds, and it's expected to be cold and windy right through the weekend. Dallas is experiencing unseasonably cold weather—forty-eight degrees.

It's raining as far east as Detroit and Toronto, and that rain is going to continue through tomorrow, when it may turn to snow. Currently forty-three degrees in Detroit, forty-one degrees in Toronto. And temperatures dropping.

It's snowing heavily in Montreal, ladies and gentlemen, its first storm of the season, and we expect that snow activity to move down from Canada into the eastern states sometime tomorrow, probably reaching the New York area sometime tomorrow night.

Good weather across the south. Clear skies in Miami, and they're going to enjoy a sunny seventy-eight degrees in that town this weekend, so if you're thinking about a vacation, now's the time to do it. Back to Chicago. Once again, continuing rain tonight through Sunday. Current temperature, thirty-eight degrees. And that winds up our weather report for this evening. This is Dave Spellman. Have a good night, and if you're going out, don't forget your umbrella.

【Section 2】

A story: What happened while the train was in the tunnel?

One day, a few years ago, a train was travelling through the English countryside. This was in the days when trains had small compartments, and in one particular compartment there were four people. There was a young girl, quite pretty, who looked like a student or someone who was starting her first job; there was an old lady, dressed in black with bags and magazines and knitting; there was an army officer in his mid-thirties, immaculately dressed in his uniform and very stiff and proper in his manner; and finally there was a young cockney, casually dressed with a sparkle in his eye and ever ready to have a joke. It was quite obvious that both the men were attracted to the young girl, though the officer certainly wouldn't show it and the cockney felt inhibited by the presence of the others.

Suddenly the train went into a tunnel; the lights had not been put on, so for half a minute the carriage was in complete darkness, and in the darkness came the sound of a large kiss followed almost immediately by a loud slap. What had taken place while the train was in the tunnel? When the train finally emerged and it was light again in the carriage, there for all to see was the officer with a bleeding nose and a swollen eye.

And the old lady, seeing this, thought to herself, "What a brave young lady, who dared to hit the officer for stealing a kiss in such a cowardly way!"

And the young girl, seeing the suffering of the officer, was puzzled. "How strange", she thought, "that the officer should kiss the old lady and not me!"

The poor officer, nursing two injuries that caused him more than a little pain and embarrassment, considered to himself, "That cockney's quite a clever chap! He kissed the girl, and the girl hit me!"

And the cockney laughed silently to himself at the trick he had played. "I am a clever chap," he thought to himself. "I kissed the back of my hand, hit the officer in the face and nobody said a word!"

【Section 3】

American government

The constitution provided for a Federal form of government with powers divided between the national and State Governments. The Federal Government is concerned with all matters that are important to the nation as a whole.

In Washington, DC, the three branches of the Federal Government have been established: the Legislative, the Executive and the

Judicial. The Legislative Branch is Congress, made up of two houses, which meet in the Capitol. The House of Representatives has members elected from each State in proportion to the population of the State. The Senate has two members elected from each State. The Executive Branch is the President, who, with his Cabinet, administers the laws. The President, elected by all the people, lives in the White House. The Judicial Branch consists of the nine judges of the Supreme Court who have the final decision as to whether or not a Congressional law or an Executive act is true to the spirit of the Constitution. Thus Congress makes the laws, the President carries out the laws and the Supreme Court interprets the laws.

Among the powers of the Federal Government are those to mint money, to tax the people, to keep an army, a navy and an air force to defend the nation, and to conduct foreign affairs. Through the Federal courts the Government also has power over the individual in cases related to the interpretation of the Federal Constitution or of laws and treaties made under it.

The State Governments retain exclusive power over all local affairs. They are self-governing units with their own governors, legislatures and courts. They pass laws on health, education, local taxes and many other important matters.

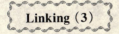

【Section 4】

Linking (3)

Part 2

2. (2) Listen to the conversation and fill in the blanks with the

words you hear.

A: What do you have in the way of wrenches?

B: We only carry that brand there.

A: Twenty dollars? That's a lot for just a wrench.

B: You want one that'll last a long time, don't you?

A: Yes, but I hadn't planned on spend that much.

B: Actually, this one'll be going on sale next week. I could give you the sale price today.

A: What kind of a discount are we talking about?

B: Twenty-five.

A: That settles it. I'll take it.

4. (1) A: She has a reputation for being a gentle dentist.

B: Don't count on it.

(2) A: If you went to work more, you'd get as A.

B: I have too many other things to get caught up on.

(3) A: Who's going to water the plants while I'm gone?

B: I'll do the honours.

(4) A: Looks like I found out a little too soon.

B: I meant it to be a surprise.

Unit 7

【Section 1】

Catching planes

(1) Last call for United Airlines flight 305 to San Francisco, departing from gate 35.

(2) This is the first call for Japan Airlines flight 29 to Tokyo, departing now from gate 16.

(3) This is the first call for Delta Airlines flight 6120 to Los Angeles, departing now from gate 23B.

(4) Announcing the departure of NorthWest Airlines flight 13 to Miami, now boarding at gate 11A.

(5) Final call for Cathay Pacific flight 300 to Hong Kong, now boarding at gate 35.

(6) This is the first call for Air France flight 603 to Paris, now boarding at gate 19B.

(7) Announcing the final call for American Airlines flight 55 to Mexico City, now boarding at gate 33A.

(8) This is the final call for British Airways flight 16 to London, now boarding at gate 25A.

【Section 2】

A trip to Los Angeles

(H for Mrs Hall, J for James)

H: Jimmy, haven't you finished packing yet?

J: No, Mom, but it's all right. There isn't much to do.

H: Well, I'll give you a hand. Oh. There isn't much room left. Is there anywhere to put your shaving kit?

J: Yeah, sure. It'll go in here. Now, I have three more shirts to pack. They'll go on top, but there's another pair of shoes to get in. I don't know where to put them.

H: Put them here, one on each side. There. OK. I think we can close it now.

J: OK. Where's the tag?

H: What tag, dear?

J: The name tag that the airline gave me to put on the suitcase. Oh, here it is.

H: Now, do you have the key?

J: What key?

H: The key to lock the suitcase, of course.

J: It's in the lock, Mom. Don't make such a production. There's nothing to worry about. There's plenty of time.

H: Have you forgotten anything?

J: I hope not.

H: And you have a safe pocket for your traveler's checks?

J: Yes, they're in my inside coat pocket.

H: Do you have a book to read on the plane?

J: Yes, it's in my briefcase.

H: What about small change to make phone calls?

J: Check. I have a pocketful of coins.

H: And is everything all arranged?

J: What do you mean?

H: Well, is there someone to meet you in Los Angeles?

J: No, Mom. I'll rent a car and go to a motel near the Orange office. They suggested the Newport Beach Holiday Inn.

H: Do you have a reservation?

J: I hope so. I asked them to make it—the motel reservation, I mean. (I reserved the car myself.)

H: Well, you've taken care of everything. I don't know why I'm worrying. Take care of yourself and be good. Call us tonight.

J: Thanks, Mom. I will.

H: Oh, I nearly forgot! Here's some gum to chew on the plane—you know, when it's coming down. It's sugarless.

J: Oh, Mom. Don't worry. I'll be all right. I'll see you next month.

【Section 3】

Parliament in Great Britain

Parliament in Great Britain is based on the principle that the people of the country hold ultimate power. They can exercise this power at least every five years, by voting for the person that they want to represent them in parliament, and by voting in a Government. The Government is made up of around 100 people from the ruling party, chosen by the Prime Minister. The most senior members of the Government are called the Cabinet.

The Government—the elected party—makes all important decisions about how the country is run. However, these decisions have to be approved by Parliament, which has the power to force the Government to change its mind when necessary.

It is the job of parliament to make sure that the Government is working properly and in the public interest. Parliament is made up of three institutions: the House of Commons, which has 651 elected representatives called Members of Parliament (or MP); the House of Lords, which is an unelected second chamber; and the monarchy:

the King or queen.

Every Member of Parliament, no matter what political party he or she belongs to, has to examine the work of the Government. The opposition, which consists of all those parties which are not part of the Government, plays the leading part in this.

【Section 4】

Reduction and contraction (1)

Part 2

1. (1) A: Care for another helping?
   B: I couldn't eat another bite.
   (2) A: Were they asking for me?
   B: I believe so.
   (3) A: Now you look happier.
   B: It helps to talk.
   (4) A: What are you going to do this weekend?
   B: Probably sleep.
   (5) A: What do you want to do about that?
   B: I'm not going to do anything.
   (6) A: A hamburger and chocolate shake.
   B: For here or to go?
   (7) A: Have you heard anything yet?
   B: No, but I have an appointment tomorrow. Maybe I'll find out more from her then.
   (8) A: Have they gone to work yet?
   B: I thought I heard his car warming up.

(9) A: Have I made myself clear?

B: Perfectly.

(10) A: have we finished all the work?

B: All that needs to be done for now.

(11) A: Has the mail come yet?

B: I just saw her go by.

(12) A: The lawn needs mowing.

B: As if he cares.

2. (1) A: Will that be cash or charge?

B: Cash—wait, I mean check.

A: Do you have a driver's license or other identification?

B: How about a driver's license and passport?

A: One or the other is OK.

B: Here you are.

(2) A: How've you been keeping since I last saw you?

B: Not so bad. I've been always, actually, I've been over to Sweden for a couple of week.

A: And you've had no problems since I last saw you?

B: None at all. No, I think everything's OK.

(3) A: How about another helping?

B: No thanks, I'm stuffed. I've had way more than I should have.

A: Won't you have any dessert?

B: No. thanks. And I'd better not had any coffee either. I haven't been sleeping so well.

A: Has anything been the matter?

B: I'm not sure. I've also been having headaches.

A: Have you seen a doctor?

B: I don't know if he could do anything for me.

A: It's worth a try.

B: I don't really like the one I have, though.

A: Go to mine. I'll give you her number.

B: Well...

A: Give her a call. You've got nothing to lose—except more sleep.

(4) A: Have you gotton caught upon your taxes?

B: No. I keep putting them off 'cause I know I'll just end up owing more.

A: I owe you a thanks. Your advice about waiting to invest my money certainly paid off. That stock I wanted to buy took a big drop.

B: I wish I had followed it myself. My finances have really taken a beating these last few months. And just as the market was starting to recover...

A: You need the luck of my grandmother. She always invests at the right time.

B: Your grandma? Are you kidding?

A: Seriously. She's the most financially secure of the family. And she's done it all on her own.

B: What do you know! To think of all the time I've spent studying investments when maybe I should have been getting to know your grandmother!

3. A: Hello, George. This is Sylvia. Can I speak to Jane?

B: Oh, hello, Sylvia. Yes, of course. She'll be with you in a minute. She's just come in and she's taking her coat off. By the way, John and Barbara called and said they're going to

Portugal next week. They said to tell you they'll be calling to see if you're all right after operation.

Unit 8

【Section 1】

Describing people

(1) A: Tell me about your boyfriend, Anne.

B: Well, his name's Bob. He's seventeen. Let me see. Well, he's got curly blond hair. He's not very tall—about average. But he's really good-looking.

(2) A: So, Bob, what's the new girl in class like?

B: She's pretty tall, about 170 centimeters. She's got glasses and short curly hair. I think she's about 20.

A: What's her name?

B: I can't remember. Anne, I think.

(3) A: It's my little boy. I can't find him.

B: Don't worry, Ma'am. We'll find him. How old is he?

A: He's seven.

B: I see. And what color is his hair?

A: It's light brown.

B: Don't worry. We'll find him for you.

(4) A: My little girl was here a minute ago, and now I can't find her.

B: She's probably in the toy section. Can you describe her?

A: Yes, she's five years old.

B: And what color hair does she have?

A: Brown. And it's very curly.

B: All right. Let's check the video screen and see where she is.

(5) A: Anyone seen a young kid?

B: How old, Sir?

A: He's ten. He's always getting lost. Drives me crazy.

B: How tall is the boy, Sir?

A: Gee. Good question. I don't really know.

B: That's OK. And what color is his hair?

A: Blond, and he wears it really long. Looks just like a girl.

(6) A: Excuse me. I've lost my daughter.

B: Is she in her teens, about average height, with short blond hair?

A: Why, yes.

B: She's looking for you—over their—in the shoe department.

A: Thanks a lot.

【Section 2】

Is only always lonely?

Are "only children" spoilt? Do parents and grandparents really give them everything they want? Zoe King, fifteen, has a good lifestyle: she's got her own TV, computer and phone. But she thinks her parents are stricter than her friends' parents. "Because I'm the only one, they always know where I am and what I'm doing. Yes, my parents can spend a lot of money on me—but they don't always. My friends with brothers and sisters often get more things—their parents don't have time to spend with them so they give them money instead."

Zoe isn't lonely because there are always friends, aunts and cousins at her home. Because they are often with older people, "only children" are usually grown-up for their age and happy to be with adults.

Zoe would like brothers and sisters. "But I know I'm more confident without them. I'm quite happy being an "only child".

Leonardo da Vinci was an "only child"—like Elvis Presley, Alexander Solzhenitsyn and Al Pacino. "Only children are often very successful in life because their parents give them a lot of love and attention and they want to do well for their parents. However, they don't have to fight with brothers and sisters to get things so they aren't competitive.

【Section 3】

Laws in Great Britain

Once MPs take their seats in parliament their most important job is to participate in parliament's main role, which is to make legislation. Every year, parliament passes about a hundred laws directly, by making Act of Parliament. Because this can be a long process, parliament sometimes passes a very general law and will leave a minister to fill in the details. In this way, it indirectly passes about 2,000 additional rules and regulations.

No new law can be passed unless it has completed a number of stages in the Houses of Commons and the House of Lords. The monarch also has to give the Bill the Royal Assent, which is now just a formality. Since the sixteenth century the monarch has never refused assent. Whilst a law is still going through parliament it is called a Bill. There are two main types of Bill—Public Bills and Private Bills.

Public Bills are the most important, as they are intended to affect the public as a whole. They can either be sponsored by the Government, when it wants to put new policies into effect, or they can be sponsored by an individual MP. These are then called Private Member's Bills and often concern moral issues.

Private Bills give particular powers of benefits to any person or body. They are intended to affect only one particular area or organization, not the whole country. The stages through which they pass are essentially the same as for Public Bills.

【Section 4】

Reduction and contraction (2)

Part 2

2. (1) ① Did(h) go?
② Is (h)e here?
③ Leave (h)er alone.
④ Give (h)im the pen.

⑤ Is (h)er work good?

(2) A: When did (h)e go there?

B: I don't know.

A: Who did (h)e talk to?

B: I don't know.

A: Have you talked to (h)im yet?

B: Yes, I have.

A: Did you ask (h)im?

B: What?

A: Did you ask (h)im who (h)e was with?

B: Yes, I did.

A: What did (h)e say?

B: He said it's none of your business.

3. (3) ① The party was great.

② We'll take a cab.

③ Here's my card.

④ They just got up.

Unit 9

【Section 1】

Asking and following directions (1)

Norm has offered to run some errands for his friend, Sandy. On the shopping list, write the places where Norm can find the items. Label the positions of these places on the map.

(N for Norm, S for Sandy)

N: Sandy, before I go out, could I go over the list and see if there's anything else you need?

S: Mm, yes. OK... looks good, that's about everything. Now, you're sure you don't mind going?

N: Nah, I don't mind at all. Matter of fact, I like grocery shopping. This'll give me a chance to get a little exercise.

S: OK, good. I really do appreciate it.

N: Oh, nothing to it. Let me just check this list. Uh... first thing is... loaf of bread. (Mm-hmm.) OK. Let's see... where do I get the bread, at the supermarket?

S: Actually, no. I would like you to go to Cantor's Bakery. They have wonderful baked goods!

N: Sounds great! How do I get there?

S: Well, it isn't far from here. None of these stores are. You just walk down my street, Willow, about a block and a half, until you get to Main Street. Then you turn right. Now, don't cross Main...

N: Don't cross Main...

S: Right, because it's on this side, almost at the corner where Willow and Main meet.

N: OK, I got it. (OK.) Next on the list says, uh... three pounds of apples.

S: Mm-hmm. Now, there's a place called Farmers Market on Main Street, where most of these stores are. It's about a block farther down from Cantor's (Farther down from Cantor's...) just, yeah, just before Bay Street. So if you go to Bay Street, You'd know you've gone too far.

N: Is it on the same side of the street as Cantor's?

S: Right. Yeah.

N: OK, I got it. Now, let's see... list says... you need a pound of cheddar cheese.

S: Yes, you can get that at Farmers Market, too, or you can just go down the street to the supermarket and get the rice, coffee, rest of the things that are on the list there.

N: Tell me how I get to the supermarket.

S: OK. Now, that's two blocks farther up on Main Street from the Farmers Market, on the opposite side of the street.

N: On the other side.

S: Right. You can't miss it. It takes up almost the entire block.

N: OK, I got that.

S: Good. Oh, um... did I put toothpaste on the list?

N: Wait a minute, let me see... um... um... Yeah. Tube of toothpaste is on the list.

S: Oh, good. Now, you can get that at the supermarket, too.

N: Hey, Sandy, you mentioned you wanted a registered letter picked up at the post office...

S: Oh yes. Uh... here's the receipt. Now, from the supermarket you should go back to Bay, then turn left, and go over on Bay one block.

N: One block. Uh-huh.

S: Yeah. On the right is the post office. It's on the corner of Bay and Fulton.

N: Hey, that sounds easy. I think I've got it straight. See you in an hour or so.

S: OK, good, and thanks, Norm. See you later.

N: No problem. See you.

【Section 2】

Jigsaw story

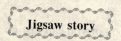

And I looked at him, and I didn't even think, I just felt so angry, just rushed at him and fell on him.

Anyway I got up, I pulled on a house dress, and I'd just pulled on my dress and turned round when the door of my bedroom opened.

He dropped the bags and managed to wriggle his coat back on, and dashed out of the flat, with me rushing after him, screaming "Stop, stop, stop."

It was someone moving in all the rooms, and very quietly. And I was rather suspicious.

Yes, we heard you shouting, but we thought it was a domestic quarrel between your two flatmates, and we didn't want to interfere.

At that time my friends started teaching in the morning before I did.

And we struggled and wrestled all the way up the corridor of the flat towards the front door, with me trying to pull off his jacket just to stop him and me trying to get the bags out of his hands.

And when I woke up I became aware of sounds in the flat and I thought at first that it was my friends who'd come back from work.

And a man stood on the threshold holding two bulging plastic bags full of cameras and tape recorders and cassettes.

And Tariq, my colleague, came to the door, and I said, "A thief, a thief in our flat, didn't you hear me shouting?"

At that time my friends started teaching in the morning before I did. And when I woke up I became aware of sounds in the flat and I thought at first that it was my friends who'd come back from work. And then I began to think the sounds were rather strange because it wasn't someone just clattering happily round, moving plates, making a noise. It was someone moving in all the rooms, um... very quietly. And I was rather suspicious. Anyway I got up, I pulled on a house dress, and I'd just pulled on my dress and turned round when the door of my bedroom opened and a man stood on the threshold holding two bulging plastic bags full of cameras and tape recorders and cassettes and any hardware that he could lay his hands on round the flat. And I looked at him, and I didn't even think, I just felt so angry, I just rushed at him and fell on him, and started trying to fight him and pull the bags away. And we struggled and wrestled all the way up the corridor of the flat towards the front door, with me trying to pull off his jacket just to stop him and me trying to get the bags out of his hands. Anyway at the door of the flat he decided to give up the struggle. He dropped the bags and managed to wriggle his coat back on, and dashed out of the flat, with me rushing after him, screaming "Stop, stop, stop," and and then banging on the nearest door er where one of our colleagues from the department lived. And Tariq, my colleague, came to the door and I said "A thief, a thief in our flat, didn't you hear me shouting?" And he said, "Oh sorry," he said, "Yes, we heard you shouting, but we thought it was a domestic quarrel between your two flatmates, and we didn't want to interfere."

【Section 3】

The family in Great Britain (1)

There are many different views on family life. Some people could not do without the support and love of their families. Others say it is the source of most of our problems and anxieties. Whatever the truth is, the family is definitely a powerful symbol. Turn on the television or open a magazine and you will see advertisements featuring happy, balanced families. Politicians often try to win votes by standing for "family values": respects for parental authority, stability in marriage, chastity and care for the elderly.

Sociologists divide families into two general types: the nuclear family and the extended family, which may include three or more generations living together. In industrialized countries, and increasingly in the large cities of developing countries, the nuclear family is regarded as normal. Most people think of it as consisting of two parents and two children. In fact, the number of households containing a nuclear family is shrinking year by year.

There are people who say that the family unit in Britain is in crisis and that traditional family life is a thing of the past. This is of great concern to those who think a healthy society is dependent upon a stable family life. They see many indications that the family is in decline, in such things as the acceptance of sex before marriage, the increased number of one-parent families, the current high divorce rate and what they see as a lack of discipline within the family.

Some politicians blame social problems, such as drug taking and juvenile crime, on a disintegrating family life.

【Section 4】

Reduction and contraction (3)

Part 2

1. (1) A: How'd you like what I fixed?
   B: I think I'd be better cooked.
   (2) A: I'll try to carpool with someone.
   B: That'd be your best bet.
   (3) A: You'll stay a little longer, wont' you?
   B: Can't. We're about to have dinner—which'll be cold if I don't hurry.
   (4) A: This room's a mess.
   B: Given the circumstances, I'd say it looks pretty good.
2. (1) A: Haven't you finished that report yet?
   B: Well no, I've not quite finished.
   (2) A: I didn't see Steve yesterday.
   B: No, he's not got back from France yet.
   (3) A: Do you think Susan has left already?
   B: No. She wouldn't have gone without telling you.
   (4) A: I'm afraid we won't be able to make it this evening.
   B: That's a pity. Could you get a baby-sitter?
3. Dear Mr Norlin,
   Thank you very much for your invitation to the Geneva conference. I'd be delighted to participate. You asked me if I'd like to

contribute a paper and, of course, I'd be very happy to do so. Unfortunately, I can't give you the final title as I haven't yet received the conference outline, but I'll send you details as soon as I can. It's a pity I didn't get to see you when I was in Paris. If I'd known you were there too, I'd've contracted you. However, I'm sure we'll see each other sometime before the conference.

Your sincerely,

P. D. Wright

Unit 10

【Section 1】

Asking and following directions (2)

A young couple is moving into a small apartment. Write the name of each piece of furniture in its correct position on the floor plan.

(M for Man, W for Woman)

M: Gee, I don't remember it being this small. I thought the room was a lot bigger.

W: So did I. But it'll be OK once we get the furniture in. Look, why don't we put the armchairs in front os the fireplace?

M: Yeah. Um, maybe we should decide really where the bed goes first. It is the biggest piece of furniture, after all...

W: Right. Well, why don't we put the bed behind the door as you come in?

M: Oh, yeah, that's a good idea. Um... we could put the bed in the corner.

W: OK. Now, what's next?

M: Well, how about the dresser?

W: Why don't we put it across from the fireplace in the corner next to the closet? I'm going to put it there now. Why don't you help me?

M: Why don't you move it and I'll just watch.

W: Oh, yeah, right. Come on, lift your end. Now, don't scratch the floor.

M: OK, but it's heavy.

W: What's in it? I thought you were supposed to empty out the drawers.

M: Well, I didn't get around to that this morning...

W: Ah... (Mm.) didn't get around to it... Let me see... how does that look?

M: It looks good.

W: Hmm, now, where do you want your desk?

M: Well, how about in the far corner between the two windows? I mean, I need lots of light.

W: Do you think it'll fit there?

M: Well, it'll probably fit if w... we can put it diagonally.

W: Oh, good idea. And then the chair can have its back to the fireplace. (Mm-hmm.) Yeah, I could live with that. All right, what about the bookcase?

M: Well, how about on the far wall between those two windows, I guess, so it'll be right near the desk?

W: Yeah, yeah, good idea. All right, where do you think the TV should go?

M: How about in the corner to the left of the fireplace, so we can watch it from the armchairs? And we can put the stereo next to the TV with, uh, the speakers on either side of the fireplace.

W: Terrific! Now, let me see, what else is there?

M: Well, there's the table lamp.

W: Well, the table lamp should go on top of the dresser. Hold it a minute, I'm... I'm trying to find the outlet.. You know, that really looks nice.

M: Mm-hmm. Looking at the desk, though, I think I may need some more light to work. Well, I could buy a desk lamp.

W: Good idea. You know, the place really looks good.

M: Yeah.

W: You want to put your books in the bookcase now, or do you...

【Section 2】

The new home

(J for Jenny, K for Karen, T for Tom)

J: You certainly do have a beautiful home. But how did you two find the time to fix it up so nicely? You've really made it look beautiful.

K: Thanks, but we needed a professional to help us. For example, we hired an architect to help us change the structure of the room.

T: Right. Karen, the architect, and I put our heads together to discuss what we wanted and what was possible. After a few meetings, we came up with some very good ideas that everybody agreed with. The architect was very good at helping us discover what could be done.

J: But it must've been pretty expensive, wasn't it?

K: Architects aren't cheap, that's for sure. But the rest of it was surprisingly inexpensive. Many times, we didn't even have to buy materials. We were able to make do with the materials we already had.

T: Yeah. For example, many of curtains we have on the window were made from bed sheets that we already had. In fact, Karen even made up some of the pillows on the couch from sheets.

J: What an interesting idea.

K: The real problem was the livingroom. It was really small and not at all special. It just looked like a box. But finally, we hit on an idea after talking about it. The architect suggested adding a fireplace. That makes the room look bigger and gives it more character. We were really happy to make that breakthrough. That solution makes the livingroom look wonderful.

T: I have to admit, we were pretty frustrated about the livingroom at first. But it's funny how people can find solutions after they kick something around for a while. Talking about it really helps.

J: Well, the fireplace is just wonderful. You worked out a beautiful solution. And I also love the windows in your diningroom. Were they here when you moved in?

T: No. That's another idea the architect thought up. She wanted to make the diningroom seem bright and charming. She said adding colored glass windows would do that for us.

J: Did you make all of these plans ahead of time?

K: Oh yes. The architect had already drawn up plans for us to approve before work began. But it's funny. No matter how much we planned, it was so exciting when the house finally started to take shape. Seeing the result was much more exiting than seeing the plans.

J: Could you tell me your architect's name? I might want to make a few changes in my house.

T: Here's her business card. She's actually just graduated recently.

J: You're kidding. Was your house her first project?

K: Yes, it was. We knew while she was a student. We wanted some work down and she needed to develop her reputation, so she used our house as a dry run. She got some extra practice, and we can show all our friends, like you, how good she was.

J: Well I'm very impressed with her work. I can't wait to talk with her and find out what wonderful things she can dream up for my house. She seems to have a great imagination. I just hope she hasn't lost her touch already. I want some of that creativity she used on your house for myself.

【Section 3】

The family in Great Britain (2)

Many people think there was once a golden age in which the world was filled with happy families. The mother ran the house, and the father went out to work to bring back enough money for this ideal family to live its life. The family —mother, father and three or four healthy, happy children—would go out for an occasional treat. Roles were very clear for the parents and children. Discipline within the family unit was strong, and moral standards were high. This image is the kind of family life people mean when they talk about "Victorian values".

It is doubtful whether many families ever lived such a life, especially in Victorian times. Working hours were long for most families, and children were often poorly fed and badly clothed. The vision of a golden age is based perhaps on how we think perfect family life should be.

What is clear about Britain in the 1990s is that it is more socially acceptable to have alternative life styles, relationships and ways of bringing up children than it has ever been. It is also easier to remove oneself from an unhappy family situation. In most social groups, divorce is no longer seen as taboo. One-parent families are common. Many children are given more freedom when young; when they move away from home, they move earlier (usually at around 18), and go further. People experiment with relationships before committing themselves to marriage. In such a multi-cultural society there are many examples of different ways of living.

【Section 4】

Sound discrimination

Part 2

1. (1) Prices these days, I ask you, shocking. Even going down to

the shops for half a pound of butter nearly breaks the old piggy bank—know what I mean? We should never've gone decimal. We should've kept the old pounds, shillings and pence.

(2) People ask what it's like to live down under and I always say the same thing. It's probably like living anywhere else but the climate's better-sun'n' surf. Just a pity it's such a long way for you Europeans!

(3) But it's a beautiful country-you've got to come over and see it for yourself! Sure, it rains but that's why it so green! And the scenery—to tell the truth, we're better off without too many tourists. It would only spoil what mother nature's given us!

(4) I guess people have this strange idea that we're convinced we're bigger and better than anyone else. I can't say for sure about better, but bigger? It sure is a big country you're talking about here. You only realize how big when you're driving from east to west!

(5) People don't always realize we've got the oldest language in Europe. Oh, they come looking for mountains and scenery. We've got plenty of that, mind you! But we've got a very old and ancient culture, and some of the best singers in the world!

2. These are the sounds. You can make your own suggestions about where you might hear them.

(1) engaged telephone signal

(2) pneumatic drill

(3) lawn mower cutting grass

(4) car brakes screeching

(5) helicopter

(6) background chatter at a party

(7) fans screaming at a rock concert

(8) washing machine spinning

(9) glass smashing

(10) a dog barking

3. (1) I'm speaking to you from the main runway where a few flights are still operating.

(2) Actually we're in an emergency phone box on the motorway.

(3) Hey! What do you think you're doing to my car?

(4) This is a staff announcement. Could Andrew Sinclair please come to the customer service desk at the front of the store?

(5) And the crowd are going wild here—with only tow minutes left to go.

(6) Go on, go on! Go and fetch it Rover!

4. (1) I mean to say, people are being **turfed out** of their **homes**-and all because the government have decided to **build** this new **link road**.

(2) Imagine taking to the skies and **floating** gently across the open country**side** in a **wicker basket**-you can see for **miles** and miles.

(3) The Bisell **Magic broom** must be **one** of the most **versatile upright vacuum cleaners** on the **market** today. It can do in seconds what it might take you **hours** to do **by hand**.

(4) The society has been in the **red** for six months now, and **auditors** say that its **financial future** looks **insecure**.

(5) During our three-day trip to **Holland**, you will be taken on a **full-day excursion** to the **Dutch bulb fields** to visit the world-**famous nurseries**.

Unit 11

【Section 1】

Finding out about a course

A student phones a college office for information about courses. Write down the answers to her questions.

A: Hello. Klarkson College. May I help you?

B: Yes. I'm looking for information on courses in computer programming. I would need it for the fall semester.

A: Do you want it day or evening course?

B: Well, it would have to be an evening course since I work during the day.

A: Uh-huh. Have you taken any courses in data processing?

B: No.

A: Oh, well, data processing is a pre-requisite course. You have to take that course before you can take computer programming.

B: Oh, I see. Well, when is it given? I hope it's not on Thursdays.

A: Well, there's a class that meets on Monday evenings at seven.

B: Just once a week?

A: Yes. But that's almost three hours, from 7 to 9:45pm.

B: Oh, that's all right. I can manage that. How many weeks does the course last?

A: Um, let me see. 12 weeks. You start the first week in September and finish...oh, just before Christmas, December 21st.

B: And how much is the course?

A: That's $ 300 and that includes the necessary computer time.

B: Uh-huh, OK. Um, where do I go to register?

A: Registration is on the 2nd and 3rd of September, between 6 and 9 pm, in Frost Auditorium.

B: Is that that round building behind the parking lot?

A: Yes, that's the one.

B: Oh, I know how to get there. Oh, is there anything I should bring with me?

A: No. Just your check book.

B: Well, thank you so much.

A: You are very welcome. Bye.

B: Bye-bye.

【Section 2】

School decisions

(A for Alice, B for Ben)

A: Have you decided what courses you're going to take next semester?

B: So far, it looks like I'm taking seven courses.

A: You can't do that. That's out of the question. It's too many courses you take at the same time.

B: I know. But I can't make up my mind. I want to take Spanish, but I also like French and German.

A: You should take into account the usefulness of each language. Spanish is very useful in the United States, so that's an important consideration.

B: Yes, but the class is already closed.

A: Then it's impossible right?

B: No. I could ask for special permission to register.

A: Good idea.

B: But a friend of mine asked for permission and the teacher turned him down. Now he has to find a different class too.

A: You know, I've always wanted to study Arabic or Chinese. Why don't we do it together?

B: Absolutely not. I draw the line at languages with difficult writing systems.

A: Ok. What else are you planning to study?

B: I need a science class, but I don't know which one.

A: Have you looked over the schedule of courses?

B: Sure, but I can't make a decision.

A: Well, only you can decide. Your schedule is up to you, not me.

B: I think I have to get rid of a couple of courses. Maybe I should take out the language and sciences classes.

A: What else do you have there?

B: English, math, history, psychology, and music. On second thought, maybe I should take Spanish instead of math.

A: You know, you can change your mind later. You don't have to make the final decision now. If you aren't happy with your choices after the semester starts, you can back out of some of the courses.

B: That's true. Maybe I should take mathematics. It's important.

A: By all means. Everyone needs mathematics.

B: I'm so confused about this. I think I'll have to talk to my advisor.

A: That's a good idea. He can help you figure out what to register for.

B: The problem is that he never lets me have a voice in my registration when I ask for his help. He tried to make the decision for me without asking my opinion.

A: Yeah. I know what you mean. Then you'd better think twice about going to him for help. It might not be a very good idea.

【Section 3】

Some of the problems facing learners of English

Today I'd like to talk about some of the problems that students face when they follow a course of study through the medium of English—if English is not their mother tongue.

The problems can be divided into three broad categories: psychological, cultural and linguistic. The first two categories mainly affect those who come to study in Britain. I'll comment only briefly on these two categories and then spend most of the time looking at linguistic difficulties which apply to everyone. Some of the common psychological problems really involve fear of the unknown: for example, whether one's academic studies will be too difficult. Looking at the cultural problems, we can see that some of them are of a very practical nature, *eg* arranging satisfactory accommodation. Others are less easy to define.

The largest category seems to be linguistic. Let's look at this in some detail. Most students, in their own countries, will have had little opportunity to practise using English. When foreign learners first have the opportunity to speak to an English-speaking person they may have shock: they often have great difficulty in understanding! I'll just mention three of the possible reasons for this.

First, it seems to students that English people speak very quickly. Second, they speak with a variety of accent. Third, different styles of speech are used. For all of these reasons students will have difficulty, mainly because they lack everyday practice in listening to English people speaking English.

What can a student do then to overcome these difficulties? Obviously, attend English classes and if a language laboratory is available use it as much as possible. He should also listen to programmes in English on the radio and TV. Perhaps most important of all, he should take every opportunity to meet and speak with native English-speaking people.

In addition, the student probably has difficulty in speaking English fluently. The advice here will seem difficult to follow but it's necessary. Firstly, he must simplify what he wants to say so that he can express himself reasonably clearly. Secondly, he must try to think in English, not to translate from his mother tongue. This'll only begin to take place when his use of English becomes automatic; using a language laboratory and listening to as much English as possible will help.

【Section 4】

Rhythm

Part 2

4. (1) Can't stop now.
   (2) Come here quick.
   (3) Come and give me a hand
   (4) That young man looks ill.
   (5) That old woman looks lovely.
   (6) Whizz gets out dirt fast.
   (7) All soap makes clothes clean
   (8) Whizz will do your washing quickly.
   (9) Don't drink tap water.
   (10) Turn the tap off.
   (11) John can't come yet.
   (12) John can't have come yet.

Unit 12

【Section 1】

Telephone message

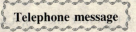

A woman is trying to phone her friend. Put a check next to the picture that best describes the message that she leaves.

(J for Jeff, P for Pat)

J: Hello?

P: Hello, is Annie there?

J: No... um... I'm sorry, she's out. I'm expecting her back in about an hour.

P: Jeff? Jeff, this is Pat.

J: Oh, hi, Pat.

P: Hi. How are you? Uh, look, could you give Annie a message for me?

J: Sure. Let me find a... a piece of paper here. Um... wait a sec...All right, I got one. Um...what's the message?

P: Well, I'm supposed to be meeting Annie for lunch at Greenbean's restaurant. Would you ask her to look and check, see if she has my French-Italian dictionary, and if she does, tell her to bring it along?

J: All right. Bring your French-Italian dictionary if she has it.

P: Right. thanks, Jeff. So, How you doing?

J: Oh, not bad. Um...my knee hurts a lot. I've been playing a lot of tennis lately but, uh, other than that, I'm fine. How are you?

P: OK. I'm busy, though. I am so busy at the office. Um...oh, gee, I almost forgot. Look, I'm running a little late this morning. Tell Annie that I can't meet her until one-thirty.

J: OK, one-thirty. (Right.) I'll tell her.

P: Good. Good. Look, I got another call on the other line. I got to go.

J: I know how that is. Take care. Bye.

P: Bye. Thanks.

【Section 2】

A dangerous woman?

It was very hot day in New York. I opened the window in my office, but it didn't help. It was still hot. I had a long cold beer. That helped. It was 10 o'clock in the morning and there were no clients. No clients means no money. I was nervous. My bank manager was nervous. I had another beer. I wasn't nervous any more. At 10:15 she walked into my office. She was blonde and she was beautiful. I didn't move. I did nothing. She sat down and took one of my cigarettes. I gave her a light. She smoked in silence. She wanted something. But what? Then she looked straight into my eyes and spoke. Her eyes were very blue—like the sea. She said, "Mr Spenser, my name's Diana White. I want your help and I can pay." She put ten thousand dollars on my desk. I was interested, very interested. I didn't speak. I waited. "Yesterday evening I arrived home very late. I was tired. I went into the bedroom. I saw a newspaper on the bed but my husband, Philip, wasn't there." I listened to her story. The story so far... Spenser is a private detective. One day a beautiful blonde woman, Diana White, went to his office. She asked for his help. She said that when she arrived home the evening before, her husband, Philip, wasn't there... "That wasn't unusual." said Diana White. "Philip's a businessman and businessmen work long hours. Anyway, I had a drink—there was a glass of water on the bedside table—and I went to bed. I felt very tired and I fell asleep immediately. I slept for a long time. When I went downstairs this morning, Philip was in the kitchen. He was dead and there was a gun next to him. The police came. They say the gun has my fingerprints on it. But Mr Spenser, I DIDN'T KILL HIM. Our marriage wasn't wonderful but it was OK. I didn't hate my husband," she said.

"Does, sorry, did your husband have any enemies?" I asked. She thought. She lit another cigarette. "Well, let's say he didn't have any friends." Then she took something out of her bag. "At least, I thought he didn't. But I found this in his wallet this morning. I didn't give it to the police." It was a photograph of a film star. She had long black hair and looked dangerous. I knew her. Her name was Divine Taylor. There was an address on the back. Diana left. My first visit was to Philip White's office in downtown New York. In his desk I found his chequebooks. There was also a note. It began: "Dear Divine, I want to finish our relationship. I know about you and Lomax. I can't give you any more money..." I heard a footstep behind me. Something hit me on the head and everything went black. When I woke up it was dark. I felt something wet and warm on my head—blood! I found a button next to me—gold. I put it in my pocket. I needed a drink. Where was Philip's fridge? I walked into the next room and turned on the light. There was a fridge but no beer. Oh, well, champagne was OK. I drank some. Then I took a taxi to Divine's house. A man answered the door. He was tall and heavy. He was wearing a white jacket with six gold buttons. Well, five, actually because one was missing.

I said, "Good evening Mr Lomax. I'd like to speak to Miss Taylor, please." We went into a big sitting room. The film star was there. She looked dangerous.

"I know that you were blackmailing Philip White. You promised not to tell his wife about your relationship if he gave you money. I know that." I said to Divine. "But why did you and Lomax kill him?"

"He wanted to tell the police that we were blackmailing him," Divine said, "so we had to kill him." "And you put his wife's fingerprints on the gun while she was asleep?" I asked.

"Yes, that was easy—a few sleeping pills in her drink."

I took my phone out of my pocket.

"That's not a good idea." Lomax said and took a gun out of his pocket.

"You did well, Spenser," he said. "But not well enough. I'm sorry, but you know too much."

At that moment I heard a shot. I thought I was dead. But Lomax fell to the floor and Divine screamed, "You!"

I turned round. It was Diana White and she had a gun in her hand. She looked pale—and very beautiful.

"I followed you here," she said. "I wanted to know the truth about my husband." It was the only time in my life that a woman saved my life—and paid me $10,000!

【Section 3】

Attitudes towards the learning of vocabulary

A recent university research project investigated the attitudes of post-graduate science students towards the learning of English vocabulary. The results were surprising. I'll mention three of them.

Firstly, most of the students think that nearly every word in English has just one meaning. This is, of course, completely contrary to the facts. A glance at any English dictionary will show this. The student will frequently find seven or eight meanings listed for "simple" words.

Why, then, have these students made such a mistake? One reason may be they're all science students. Scientists try to use words in their special subject which have one meaning, and one meaning only. Another reason, of course, could be the way in which these students were taught. They may have used vocabulary lists when they first learned English. On one side of the page is the word in English; on the other side, a single word in the student's native language.

The second attitude that emerged from the findings is equally mistaken. Practically all the students think that every word in English has an exact translational equivalent. Again, this is far from the truth. Sometimes one word in English can only be translated by a phrase in the student's native language. There are other difficulties in translation which we won't mention here. Certainly the idea of a word translation process is completely false. Translation machines, which tried to work on this principle, failed completely.

The third result of the investigation showed another error in the students' thinking. They believe that as soon as they know the meaning of a word, they're in a position to use it correctly. This is untrue for any language but is perhaps particularly false for English. The student has to learn when to use a word as well as to know what it means. Some words in English mean almost the same but they can only be used in certain situations.

What, then, is the best way to increase one's vocabulary? This can be answered in three words—observation, imitation and repetition.

【Section 4】

Basic sentence stress

Part 2

3. (1) Chris, can you contact Mrs Williams before five o'clock? It's urgent.

   (2) Look Chris, I need the report on Wednesday.

   (3) Could you send the invoice to the Accounts Department, please, Chris?

   (4) Chris, I'm afraid I can't go to the meeting on Friday. I'm too busy.

4. A: In fact, even in the Soviet Union they have the same problem they've got now, in fact, er... there's a divorce for every three marriages.

   B: So is it true then if you're talking about different cultures that perhaps something like religion doesn't come into this...?

Unit 13

【Section 1】

Eating out

Dialogue 1

A: Are you ready to order?

B: Yes, I'd like to start with the salad, please.

A: OK. And what would you like for your main dish?

B: Mm. I'll have the spaghetti. Is it good?

A: I've never tried it. Anything to drink?

B: Tea, please.

A: And how about dessert?

B: Not today, thanks.

Dialogue 2

A: Hi there. What can I get you today?

B: Well, let me see. I'll just have some soup and a salad.

A: Sure. Soup and salad. Our special today is grilled fish and that comes with broccoli or peas.

B: No. Thanks. Not today. I'm not very hungry. But I would like some chocolate ice cream for dessert.

A: Sure. Anything to drink?

B: Coffee...and some water, please.

【Section 2】

An arranged marriage

Task 2

You will hear an interview with a member of the Sikh community in Britain, who talks about the idea of arranged marriage. Before you listen, work with your partner and write down any questions you would like to ask him about arranged marriage. Listen to the tape and check out how many of your questions have been answered.

A: We were neighbours, our parents knew each other very well, we went to the same schools, taught by the same teachers, played in the garden and around, and it was only later on, many years later on, when our parents thought it was a good idea to bring us together. But we weren't dragged into marriage, we had the option to say no, from my point of view there was no objection. I think Gurmit had a slightly different view, but as far as I'm concerned it's worked out very well. People perhaps have got a distorted view of arranged marriages. No partner is dragged into a marriage, we have complete freedom to say no or yes. Equally if some, if children come up with the option, then the parents have equal option to say yes or no whether they like it.

B: With your marriage, the idea though came from the parents?

A: The idea came from Gurm. It's mother. That's how she approached my mother, and both of them decided yes perhaps it is. We are of similar age, have slightly different hobbies and outlooks, but it's worked very well.

B: And what would be the, in an arranged marriage like this, what would be the important thing in deciding on a suitable partner for you, would it be social background or age or...?

A: Certainly, because one of the main things first, before any couple is introduced to each other, the parents will do a fair amount of research about the, if it's the bride's family they will certainly do a research on the bridegroom's family side, what's the family like in terms of general behaviour, their wealth, what's their standing in the society, what's the bridegroom education like, he is working or not, how well he is off, really. Because at the end of the day any parent is interested in seeing that their daughter does settle down in a well-established family.

B: In your case in fact you knew each other as children (We knew each other as children). But in other cases where the couple doesn't know each other, isn't there a danger that they, they get married-they don't have much chance to get to know each other before marriage? Is that right or...?

A: Yes, that is quite possible, yeah.

B: So isn't there a danger that they then discover that in fact they don't like each other very much?

A: Now you have to, it's like going on a course, isn't it? On an educational course, you may not like it but attending the class and learning to live with it, learning to acquire the knowledge and then use it to your benefit, you have to give and take.

B: Well, I think what very often happens now in England, say, is that a couple meet, and they get to know each other (Yeah), and then maybe at a later stage they introduce their partner to the parents. And I think a very common attitude is that, well it's not the parents who are getting married, it's the children who are getting married so they should decide. What do you think about that?

A: Um, I think parents have had, parents generally have perhaps a better experience than the children. I think they probably don't give them the same amount of credit perhaps that is due. As I said, no parent wants to see their children's marriage sort of break up, so certainly in our society, in the Asian society, they will go to great lengths to make sure that the couples are suitable, even before they're introduced. If you look at from the bridegroom's side, once he has a job and he's settled, might have his own house or he's nearly ready to own his own house, the parents would be encouraging him to get married. Obviously if he knows someone then the situation is a little easier. If not, then they would sort of pass the word within the family group that they are looking for a bride, you see. So that's how the system works. And an introduction is then sort of arranged, and at any stage if the situation doesn't look right it can be called off. It can be called off by parents or by the couple involved.

B: I think for a lot of young people in the West, the main idea that they'd have in their minds would be falling in love and being in love (Yes). And you'd fall in love with somebody and then this would be your partner. What do you think of this? Is this very superficial, do you think?

A: I think it is very superficial. I think that love comes out of a relationship really. Your initial thoughts may be you like somebody because they look right, they probably dress right, they are to the right level of education, may have the right sort of financial background, there could be many aspects which starts a relationship. And it obviously depends how the couple work at that relationship to make that relationship work. And and the tolerance to give and take comes out of that relationship.

Task 3

Gurmit and I knew each other as children. Gurmit's mother approached my mother both of them decided the marriage. We are of similar age, have slightly different hobbies and outlooks, but it's worked very well.

Before any couple is introduced to each other, the parents will do a fair amount of research about the general behaviour, the education background, the family's wealth and their standing in the society.

I think parents have had a better experience than the children. No parent wants to see their children's marriage break up. They would choose a partner for their children and once it is arranged their children still have complete freedom to say no and can call off the arrangement either by parents or by the couple involved.

I think love comes out of a relationship. Once a relationship starts, you have to use it to your benefit, you have to give and take and to be tolerant.

【Section 3】

Effective reading

When a teacher recommend a student to read a book it's usually for a particular purpose. The book may contain useful information or it may be invaluable for the ideas that it puts forward, etc. The teacher may just refer to a few pages and not the whole book.

Unfortunately, when many students pick up a book to read they tend to have no particular purpose in mind. Often they open the book and start reading slowly and in great detail. The result is that students frequently don't have an overall view of what they are reading.

Students can make their reading much more effective by adopting a plan aimed at helping them to understand and to remember what they read. Firstly, they should decide precisely why they're reading the book: perhaps it is to understand a difficult idea or argument. Then they should decide exactly what they're going to read: a chapter of a book, for example.

It's helpful to get an overview of the contents before starting to read. That can be done by reading the introduction and the conclusion, and possibly skimming (or reading very quickly) some sections in order to get a general idea of the contents.

Finally, students should ask themselves a specific question about their reading. They should then try to answer it by making notes as they read. This will help them to focus on the purpose of the reading as well as providing a summary which can be read again later. This is, perhaps, the most effective part of the reading strategy.

If a student puts into practice everything that's been suggested so far, can we say that he reads efficiently? Well, we must remember that most students have a lot to read and only a limited time in which to read it. As a result, it's important that a student reads as quickly as possible. He should aim to improve both his slowest speed, which is for detailed study, and his fastest (or skimming), which is for getting a general idea.

【Section 4】

Sentence focus (1)

2. (1) When did you arrive here?

   (2) Where did you get your English book?

   (3) Who told you how to get a visa?

   (4) What language can you speak?

   (5) Which language is the most difficult to learn?

   (6) Do you think it is hard to speak or to hear a foreign language?

3. (1) A: I've lost my **hat**. (basic stress pattern: the content word is focused)

   B: What **kind** of that? ("hat" is now an new idea; "kind" is the new focus)

   A: It was a **sun** hat.

   B: What **colour** sun hat?

   A: It was **white**. White with **stripes**.

   B: There was a white hat with stripes in the **car**.

   A: **Which** car?

   B: The one I **sold**.

   (2) A: Hello. What's **new**?

   B: **Nothing much**. What's new wity **you**?

   A: I'm going to **the States**.

   B: **East** coast or **West** coast?

   A: **West**. I want to visit **San Francisco.**

(3) A: Are you going on **holiday**?

B: No. I'm going to **study.**

A: Study **what**? **Maths** or **English**?

B: **Neither.** I'm **sick** of maths and English. I'm going to study **engineering. Electronic engineering**.

4. (1) A: **What** are you **doing**?

B: I **came** to **see Peter.**

A: Well, **Peter's not here.**

B: I can **see** he's not here. Where **is** he?

A: I don't know **where** he is.

B: **Not** very **friendly, are** you?

A: **Neither** are **you** .

(2) A: Do you think American food's **expensive**?

B: Not **really**.

A: Well, **I** think it's expensive.

B: That's because you eat in **restaurants.**

A: Where do **you** eat?

B: At **home**.

A: I didn't know you could cook.

B: Well, actually I **can't**. I just eat **bread** and **Coke.**

A: That's **awfully**!

B: No, it **isn't**. I **like** bread and Coke.

A: You're **crazy**!

Unit 14

【Section 1】

Fast food survey

A: Excuse me, do you mind answering a few questions?

B: No.

A: Um firstly, do you ever eat fast food?

B: Es, yes, I do.

A: What kind of fast food do you normally eat?

B: Oh, er you know, burgers, sandwiches, well sometimes like a pizza or, you know, kebabs.

A: Oh, right. And how often do you eat fast food? Everyday, more than once a week or less than once a week?

B: Er, well Monday to Friday when I'm working er, yeah every day, um but not not usually at the weekends.

A: And what time of day do you eat fast food?

B: Well, at work as I said, you know at lunchtime, um you know sort of go out and get a burger or a sandwich. Sometimes, you know, if if I'm gong out and I've no time to cook in the evenings then I'll, I'll send out for a pizza.

A: Ho, right. So you only eat it as a main meal or do you snack between meals?

B: No, only as a main meal, you know lunch or, or in the evening.

A: And what do you think of fast food? Which statements do you think are true? Um, either "It's convenient"?

B: Ho, definitely. I mean, that's sort of the main reason that I eat it.

A: Right. How about "It tastes good"?

B: Yeah. Um, I mean, not as good as food like in a, in a good restaurant, but it's not bad.

A: "It's good for you"?

B: No. Sort of eating quickly and standing up it's sort of bad for you. The food itself isn't very good for you, you know there's not enough greens, um you know vegetables or salad.

A: Mm. How about "It's an expensive way of eating"? What do you think of that?

B: Oh, yes, it is, er but you're paying for the convenience, you know the speed of it. Er, well, I certainly think that it's cheaper than you know cooking your own food.

A: Er, and what about lastly "It creates litter". So you think that's true?

B: Yes, yes, it does. Only I, I always put mine in a you know in a litter bin, but er unfortunately a lot of people don't, um but in the packaging there is a lot of paper involved and plastic and sometimes polystyrene.

【Section 2】

Caring for nature and culture

(K for Kate, J for Jean)

K: Jean, why is it important to protect nature?

J: Well, the answer is very simple. Unless we protect nature, many wonderful places, animals and plants will disappear.

K: I see. What are the different kinds of problems for natural sites?

J: Well, there are five main kinds of natural sites...

K: I expect sites with wild animals are important, aren't they?

J: Yes, there are many sites all around the world which are the home of large numbers of wild animals...

K: ...and unless we protect the home of those animals, they will have nowhere to live.

J: Absolutely.

K: And what about endangered animals or species?

J: Yes, we also need to protect the habitat of endangered species. Unless we stop hunting or pollution in those areas, many animals will disappear forever.

K: So, is it only animals that you want to protect?

J: Oh, no. We also need to protect places if they are beautiful.

K: You mean, places that have a fantastic view or a beautiful landscape.

J: Yes, that's right. Unless we protect beautiful places, someone might, for example, build a factory or a new road there. Other natural places are important geologically. They give us information about how the earth developed...

K: ...you mean volcanoes, for example.

J: That's right. These places give us information about how the world developed and so we have to protect them from, for example, air pollution.

K: So that's zoology—animals, geology—the earth itself. What about biology—is that important?

J: Well, yes, botany is important. Some natural places are important because particular plants, trees or flowers live there.

K: So unless we protect some plants we will have fewer and fewer plant species in the world.

J: True!

K: Thank you, Jean. That's all very interesting.

※ ※ ※

K: Is it difficult to decide which places should belong to the World Heritage Organization?

J: Yes and no! We have prepared a list of questions we can ask about special places...

K: I see. So you're looking at certain characteristics that famous places must have?

J: Yes, more or less.

K: So, what kinds of questions do you ask about historical, man-made sites?

J: I suppose there are four key questions. The first question we ask is: Is the place authentic? Is it real?

K: What do you mean by "authentic"?

J: Well, we are interested in places which are not an imitation or a copy of another place.

K: I see.

J: The reason for this is that if we lost an imitation of a place, we could build another one...

K: But if we lost an authentic place, it would be impossible to replace it.

J: Yes, that's right.

K: Good, so a place should be authentic. Anything else?

J: Then, we ask: Has this place influenced other buildings in the same country or even in another country?

K: So, it might be the first of its kind?

J: Yes, exactly. Or the best example of a certain style or design.

K: Hmm. Any other questions?

J: Yes, there are. We also ask if a place is linked with an important religion or a philosophy.

K: So this includes mosques, churches, synagogues, temples?

J: Yes, absolutely.

K: And the final question?

J: Places which are a very special example of a traditional way of life, an ancient culture or civilization are very important. If we lost a site like that we should find it difficult to understand that culture.

K: That's all very interesting. Thank you.

【Section 3】

Problems of writing in a foreign language

Learners of English usually find that writing is the most difficult skill they have to master. Even native-speakers of English often find it difficult to write well on their special subject. It may, therefore, be helpful to analyse, the types of error that the learner of English usually makes. Three broad types can be distinguished. They'll be discussed in order of importance.

The first type of error is the error which leads to a misunderstanding or even worse, to a breakdown in communication. The causes of these misunderstandings and breakdowns are numerous. We can only try to cover the most important here. Firstly, the student tends to work out a sentence in his own language and then tries to translate it word by word into English. This often produces non-English sentence patterns. Secondly, the student may confuse grammatical pattern which are similar in form but very different in meaning. Thirdly, he may choose to write sentences which are too long and complex instead of simpler ones which he can handle more easily. Finally, he may produce a phrase instead of a sentence, with the result that the reader doesn't know what it refers to.

The second type of error is the error which leads to ungrammatical English, but which doesn't usually interfere with the meaning. The wrong selection of a verb tense often comes into this category. Other mistakes which feature prominently here are really slips. If the student checks his work carefully, he can correct them himself. When he writes, therefore, he should prepare several drafts.

The third type of error concerns style and usage. When a student writes "The results of the research were terrific", he's making this type of mistake. Native speakers of English would understand but, of course, they'd never use the word "terrific" in their own academic writing.

【Section 4】

Sentence focus (2)

Part 2

1. A: Good **morning**. May I **help** you?

   B: Yes, I'd like to speak to Mr **Williams**, please.

   A: What's your **name**, please?

   B: John **Ribble**.

   A: Mr Williams. There's a Mr **Riddle** to see you.

   B: Excuse me not **Riddle**, **Ribble**.

   A: Oh, sorry. There's a Mr **Ribble** to see you, Mr Williams.

2. (C for Customer, W for Waiter) C: Can I have **one cheese sandwich** and **two ham rolls**, please?

   W: That's **one** ham sandwich...

   C: No, one **cheese** sandwich.

   W: Sorry, that's **one** cheese sandwich and **two ham** sandwiches.

   C: No, two ham **rolls**.

   W: Right...You did want **two** cheese sandwiches, didn't you?

   C: No, I **didn't**. Just **one**.

   W: Oh. I think I'd better **write** this **down**.

3. (P for Policeman, R for Rephy)

   (1) P: Now Miss, do you **usually** go to the bank on Friday?

   R: Yes, **every** Friday.

   (2) P: Did you **see** the robbers?

   R: No, but I **heard** them.

   (3) P: And did you sound the alarm?

   R: No, some one **else** did.

   (4) P: Were there three man?

   R: No, I think there were two.

4. (1) A: I didn't goon Friday.

   B: You didn't go?

(2) A: He's been promoted.

B: Promoted?

(3) A: I found your keys in the kitchen.

B: In the kitchen?

(4) A: Have you seen my purse anywhere?

B: Your purse?

(5) A: The France/Scotland match has been postponed?

B: Postponed?

5. (B for Barbara, P for Paul)

B: Hello, Paul. Did you have a good holiday?

P: Yeah, it was great.

(1) B: I **thought** you'd have a nice time.

P: Mm...ended up in Italy though.

(2) B: I thought you were going to **Spain**

P: Yeah, but Jane doesn't like Spain much.

(3) B: But I thought you were going with Maria.

P: Well, it got a bit difficult.

(4) B: Mm, I rather **thought** there might be a problem.

P: So anyway, I went to Florence.

(5) B: I thought you'd **been** there.

P: Yes, I have but I like it. Anyway, I speak the Language, you know.

(6) B: Yes, I **thought** you spoke Italian.

P: Well, I must be going, Barbara. We must have a drink together sometime soon.

(7) B: Yes, but I thought you were coming to my **party** on Saturday.

P: Oh, of course, I almost forgot. See you on Saturday then.

Unit 15

【Section 1】

Palm reading

Speaker 1

Well, you've got a very interesting hand, in fact. Um, it looks as though you're a very determined character. Um, you've got a very strong head line, um your heart line goes down quite a lot, there's quite a strong connection between the two, so I think there either have been or will be two women in your life. And it looks as though during your early life um you either were ill or you changed your mind about the way, the direction in which your life was going to go. Um, it looks to me as though you're a fairly artistic person, um, yes, I would, I would say very artistic.

Speaker 2

Now let's have a look at your hand here. Now you've got a very square, very practical hand, so you're somebody who's not afraid of hard work. On the other hand, you've got a very strange line of imagination with lots of little, little wrinkles, little valleys coming off it, which means that you're also a very imaginative person as well as being very practical. Coming down here from just above your thumb is your, is your life line. And it starts off in a little, little vaguely, it's not a very well defined line and this I think would indicate that at the beginning of your life you weren't very sure where you wanted to go, what you wanted to do, but then gradually when you got to about your twenties, I would say, you suddenly take off in this direction very, very firmly indeed, and this goes right on, I think this would, would tell me that you're going to go on in your present career until you retire at actually I have to tell you quite an early age. And just coming out of that line and going right across your hand, you've got, it's probably what we would call endeavour and determination, and I have to tell you that this again is a line that is not very firm and deep, it's a little bit vague and a little bit wavy, and I think that means that you're somebody who questions themselves a lot and is never absolutely sure that what they're going to do is right or not. And that doesn't get better as you go through life.

【Section 2】

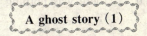

A ghost story (1)

(S for Stephanie, R for Rob)

S: This particular incident happened while my husband and I were living with friends in an old house in Highgate, in north London, and we had this large bedroom. And at one end of the room I also had a desk where I used to do my work. I could never really explain it but I often had this strange feeling that I was being watched... and... I started talking to myself... in my head, not out loud, saying "Oh, don't be silly, there's nobody there there's nothing at all." And I carried on having this feeling, so I began to talk actually out loud, saying "Now, come on, I know you're there, don't worry, just don't bother me." And the same would happen while I was working, I would suddenly feel that someone was there, and once I'd talked to it, it was OK.

R: Did you tell Jeremy this? Did he know about it?

S: Yes, I'd told him, but he didn't believe me. You see, I'd had one or two strange experiences before, when I was a child, but Jeremy just said that I was imagining things and that it was all nonsense. Anyway, we were lying in bed one night, and suddenly we both woke up, and there was somebody standing at the bottom of the bed, this figure, and we presumed it was John, one of the friends we were living with, who wanted something. So we said "What's the matter, what do you want?", and there was no answer...

R: (nervous laugh)

S: So er... I said "It's not John, it doesn't look like John". It was this tall figure. I put the light on, and.... there was nothing there...

R: But you both saw it?

S: Oh yes, we both saw it, not just me. We got up and checked. The door was closed, so goodness knows what it was. Then a few days later, Jeremy woke me up in the middle of the night. You see, in this room, we had lots of posters up on the walls, and also lots of postcards of art and pictures, and I had these postcards stuck on boards, about fifteen postcards to a board... He woke me up... it was freezing cold... each picture was falling off the wall... one by one... from left to right around the room. And when Jeremy woke me up, he was absolutely petrified...

About half the pictures were on the floor, and each one dropped off one by one, all the postcards...off the board...and then the board and then the next board...

R: What!

S: And it went right round the room, until every single piece of paper was on the floor or the bed. We were sitting in bed covered in pieces of paper, absolutely terrified of what was going to happen next.

A ghost story (2)

R: And what did happen?

S: No, that was it.

R: That was enough!

S: Yes. We got up, had a cup of tea, and tried to explain to the others the next day. They just thought we were crazy. Anyway, I still went on talking to this thing, and by this time Jeremy was convinced that there was something very strange going on...

R: You're not kidding!

S: Another night he woke up, felt there was something there, which was unusual, because he's so down to earth, it's not like him at all. And he wanted to know what this thing was. He didn't know much about contacting spirits, but knew people tried to ask them questions, so he said out loud, "When I ask a question, make a sign, any sign, to show me that you're there, once for yes and twice for no." He didn't really expect anything to happen, so anyway he asked a question out loud, "Is anybody there?"

R: Just like in the films!

S: Right. Suddenly I started breathing really deeply... and then... he told me later... my head... jerked... really strongly... once...

R: (gasp)

S: Well, he thought, "Well, it could be coincidence," and he... er... he asked another question and said, "Are you a man?" and again my head jerked once... in my sleep. And the next question after that was "Do you live in this house?" and again the answer was "Yes". And by this time Jeremy couldn't stop, because he wanted...

R: Yes.

S: ... to test it out... and he was thinking... "Let's find out..." and of course I was unconscious, This is what he told me later. I don't think he would have imagined it though, knowing him. Anyway, the next thing that happened was, he asked it various questions and the same thing would happen, my head jerked once if the answer was "Yes" and twice if the answer was "No". And he... er, well he found out that it was a man. It lived there when the house was built, it had been built for him in the early nineteenth century, and in fact that it... had been his room, and that's why he came there... he wasn't an unhappy spirit... I mean, I never really felt frightened by him, just the experience of something happening. And Jeremy established that he was really quite a happy spirit, and he was just around the house and had been all the time, and he was on his own in the house...

【Section 3】

Importance of questions

In order to obtain full value from a group discussion, a student must be good at asking questions. If he isn't, then any attempt he makes to resolve his difficulties may lead to further confusion.

A very frequent source of misunderstanding in a discussion is, in fact, the teacher's uncertainty whether his student has, indeed, asked a question at all. What often happens is as follows. The student, puzzled about a particular point, decides to ask a question. Unfortunately he concentrates all his attention on the subject matter and none on the language. Consequently, he fails to employ the correct grammatical form. The result is predicable. The teacher interprets the intended question as a comment. He either agrees or disagrees with it, or he continues with what he was saying before.

However, even when the student does employ an appropriate question form, difficulties may still arise. The teacher may not know, for example, the source of the student's difficulty. The student may not have clearly heard what was said; or he may not have understood the English that his teacher employed; or he may not have worked out the meaning of a point in relation to his special subject. Each of these difficulties requires a different kind of question.

Next, a student must ensure that his teacher is clear about exactly which point he is referring to. In order to be absolutely precise, it's a good idea for students to preface their questions with an introductory statement, for example, "I don't understand the point you made at the beginning of the discussion about cost inflation.

Could you explain it again please?" The teacher is then in a position to give a satisfactory answer without any waste of time. Furthermore, when a student asks questions on a text he must be very careful to locate the exact point.

Finally, it should be mentioned that it's often necessary to employ a question form because not to do so would be rude.

【Section 4】

Functions of intonation (1)

Part 2

1. (A for Alan, L for Louise)

(1) A: Turn slightly toward me. Your head slightly towards me.

L: Right?

A: No—only slightly towards me. Just a bit further to the right. Close to the wall. I mean to my right, not so close. Lift your face up, like that. Not right up. Not quite like that. You look a bit tease. How about a smile? I know you feel tense. Can you make it a more natural smile? You needn't look tense. Exactly as you were before. Exactly as you were before.

3. (1) They hired a **car**.

(2) No, the **train** was delayed.

(3) The bank's on the **corner**.

(4) I sent him a **letter**.

(5) It's next **Tuesday**.

Unit 16

【Section 1】

Party games

Game A

There's a game called "Hunt the thimble", where one person goes out of the room, and then so-um somebody else hides a thimble, and the person has to come in and look for it. Um, and once they've found it, they just have to choose a different person. And it can be really anywhere where you hide the thing, s long as it's in one room.

Game B

There's this party game called "Eat the chocolate". And everyone sits down in a circle, and there's a dice, and in the middle of the circle there's plate with a piece of chocolate, quite a large piece. And um there's a hat, pair of gloves, a scarf and a jacket which are placed in the middle of the circle as well. And each person gets a turn at throwing the dice. And if they get a six, they get dressed up in the hat, gloves, scarf and jacket, and they get to eat the chocolate, but they have to use a knife and fork. And sometimes they don't get enough time because the next person throws a six.

Game C

Well, everyone sits in a circle, and a bowl of eggs is put in the middle. Now half of these eggs are raw, and half of them are hard-boiled. And one by one everybody stands up and they have to crack this egg on their head very hard. And of course if it's raw it'll go all over them, but if it's hard-boiled then they'll be fine and they just sit back down. If you don't like getting messy, of course, then you can wear a towel round your shoulders and a bath cap on your head to keep your hair from getting all wet.

Game D

Well, you get in partners, and you have er two or one roll of toilet paper to each partner, and then you have a certain amount of time. And then everyone wraps one person up in toilet paper. And the first person that gets it all done, they win, and the neatest person. But if it's not neat then they don't win and it's the second person down.

【Section 2】

Friendship (1)

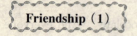

(M for Mary, D for Debbie)

M: You must be excited to be starting a new life.

D: Yeah, but nervous too. A completely new city is a big change in my life.

M: I'm sure you'll like San Francisco. I hope you plan to keep in touch with all of us.

D: Sure. I'll write and telephone as often as I can. I'm not planning to give you the cold shoulder after I get married. I'll still communicate with all of you.

M: We're counting on it.

D: Actually, I'm a little worried about making new friends in San Francisco. It's such a big city. I might be lonely there.

M: No, I'm sure you won't have any trouble meeting people and making friends. You get along with people very well. You're a very friendly person. You shouldn't worry so much.

D: I hope you're right. By the way, I forgot to give you my new address.

M: That's right. I need to know how to get in touch with you after you move. The last thing I want is to be cut off from my best friend. I'll need your letters and phone calls.

D: (laughing) I feel sorry for myself. Nobody else will put up with my bad jokes. You're the only one who ever laughs at my jokes.

M: My jokes have always been terrible too. As joke tellers, we're in the same boat, I'm afraid. We both tell terrible jokes.

D: Promise me that we won't lose touch with each other, bad jokes included.

M: I promise to write and call often. And I promise to take good care of your cat, too.

Friendship (2)

(J for Jim, B for Bod)

J: We're finished. I don't ever want to talk to you again.

B: What did I do?

J: You double-crossed me, that's what. I told you I was going to apply for that computer programming job, and you applied before me.

B: I didn't think you were sure about applying. You always say things you don't mean. I didn't take you at your word this time.

J: I just can't get through to you. How can I make you understand that I wanted that job?

B: Your mother told me that you didn't really want it.

J: That's crazy. She would never say that. She knows that's not true. You're just trying to cause trouble. You're trying to come between my mother and me.

B: You're the one who's crazy. You've never been able to control your anger.

J: Now you're attacking me. I can't believe you're putting me down like this. It's so insulting.

B: Look. It doesn't matter. We might as well make up because neither of us got the job. So we can just stop arguing.

J: What?

B: The new assistant got it.

J: But he has no experience. That's not fair.

B: I know that. We've been had. That job shouldn't have gone to him. The company cheated us again.

J: Well, we have to fight this.

B: How?

J: Let's sit down and make a plan to...

【Section 3】

Group discussion

Today I'd like to talk about group discussions. In an academic context these are often known as "seminars" and "tutorials". Firstly, I want to consider the meaning of these terms, then look at the aims of group discussions and finally I'll mention some of the problems learners of English may have in work of this kind.

Firstly, then, the meaning of the terms "seminar" and "tutorial". Originally there were clear differences in size and in purpose between a "seminar" and "tutorial'. A tutorial was usually for two to five students whereas a seminar was attended by about ten to fifteen. In a tutorial a lecturer asked and answered questions related to his recent lecture where as an introduction to a more general discussion. However, nowadays these terms are often employed interchangeably. Therefore the term "group discussion" will be used for both.

Turning now to the general aims of group discussions. I want to mention the two most important objectives. The main aim is that (and I quote from a survey) "students should be helped to discuss and to clarify difficulties arising from lectures or other teaching sessions." During a lecture students aren't usually expected to interrupt to ask questions. The second objective is, and I quote again, "to obtain more intimate and personal contact with students than is possible in lectures". In smaller groups this is, of course, much easier.

Group discussions, if they're properly exploited by students, can be highly stimulating and extremely beneficial. Yet it's difficult, especially for non-native speakers, to take full advantage of them. There are many reasons for this. I'll just mention three which I think are particularly important. Firstly, this dialogue which takes place may be very fast. Secondly, a student may not know how to break into a discussion politely. The third major difficulty is how to formulate questions quickly and accurately.

【Section 4】

Functions of intonation (2)

Part 2

2. (L for Lisa, T for Tony)

(1) L: Hello, Tony. Did you go for your interview yesterday?

T: Hi, Lisa. Yes, I did.

L: How did it go?

T: All right, I think.

L: All right? You don't sound very sure.

T: I mean I managed to answer all the questions and I think I said the right thing. But I don't think I wore the right clothes.

L: Well, there's no point in worrying about it. What's alone is done.

T: Yes, Lisa. I know there is nothing I can do about it, of course. I can't change anything, but I can't help thinking about it.

L: I'm sure you needn't worry. What did you wear anyway?

T: I had put my jeans on.

L: Your jeans? Oh, I see.

T: But I wore a tie.

L: Never mind. You said the right things anyway.

3. (1) I met Robert this morning.

(2) He told me he's in love.

(3) She's started to worry about her exams.

(4) I learned spanish at school.

4. (1) When we've finished lunch we'll look at the photos.

(2) Your use of intonation can change the meaning.

(3) The hotel was very good.

(4) You can go if you're finished.

Unit 17

【Section 1】

What sort of shop are they in?

(1) A: Good morning.

B: Gook morning. I'd like to cash this, please.

A: How would you like it?

B: Erm... Could I have some fives and a few one pound coins, please?

A: Certainly.

A: Thanks.

(2) A: Can I help you?

B: Yes. I'd like some Cheddar.

A: Is it for cooking?

B: No, it's to have with biscuits.

A: Then I recommend this one. It's mature, and quite strong.

B: Could I try a little, please?

A: Yes, of course.

B: Mmm, very nice. I'll have half a pound, please.

A: Anything else, sir?

B: No, that'll be all, thank you.

(3) A: I'd like some nice lamb chops, please.

B: English or New Zealand?

A: Is there much difference in price?

B: The New Zealand is a little cheaper, but of course it's not quite the same quality.

A: Could I have a look at the New Zealand?

B: Of course.

A: They look fine. Six please.

B: Two pounds thirty, please.

A: Thank you.

(4) A: I like the style very much, and they're very comfortable.

B: Yes, they fit extremely well.

A: I'm afraid I don't like the colour. Have you got something a bit brighter? Brown is such a dull colour.

B: I'll have a look. What about a red?

A: Yes, I've got quite a few things that might go with red. Could I try them on?

B: Yes, I'll just fetch them. One moment.

(5) A: Good morning.

B: Hello. A large wholemeal loaf, please.

A: Thank you. 57p, please.

B: And a half-a-dozen soft white rolls.

A: Do you want the ones with sesame seeds?

B: They're for hamburgers, so yes, that'd be all right, wouldn't it?

A: Yes.

B: Yes, that's fine.

A: Anything else?

B: No, thanks. Not today.

(6) A: Hello, Tom. How are you today?

B: Not bad, thanks. You?

A: OK. What can I do for you?

B: I'd like some sprouts, Alf, please.

A: I couldn't get any today. Sorry.

B: Oh. Well, I'll have some beans, then.

A: How many?

B: A pound will do. Have you got any avocados?

A: Lovely ones. When are they for?

B: Tonight, please.

A: Here we are. Two beauties.

B: A lettuce and a cucumber, please.

A: Right.

B: That's it, thanks.

(7) A: Hello. Have you got any of that stuff for getting stains out of furniture?

B: Yes. Do you mean that sort that comes in bottles? Do you want large, small or medium?

A: Oh, just the small one please.

B: 75p, please.

A: And I need some nails, some six-inch nails.

B: They come in packs of twenty-five, sir.

A: But I don't want that many. Can I just have a few?

B: I'm sorry, I can't split them up.

A: All right, then, I'll have the packet.

(8) A: Twenty Benson and Hedges, please.

B: King size?

A: No, just the ordinary ones. Oh, and some matches please.

B: There you are.

A: Do you have any computer magazines?

B: Yes, they're over there on the middle shelf.

A: Ah, yes.

【Section 2】

The best way to learn English

(L for Luis, Y for Yukiko, X for Xing, G for Giovanni)

L: Do you ever try to learn English by watching TV?

Y: Sometimes. But they talk so fast that I can't make out the words. It's much too hard to understand.

X: I know what you mean. I never get the jokes in the comedies. People in this country have a strange sense of humor.

L: But sometimes I can figure out some of the phrases and idioms, so I seem to be learning.

Y: I had to watch TV here for weeks before I started to catch onto the pronunciation. Everyone speaks so fast on TV that I didn't know what I was listening to.

G: I'm lucky. I have an American roommate. When I don't understand something, he usually fills me in. He knows how to explain very clearly.

X: TV is good for learning English because I can sometimes pick up on the meaning of words by watching the people's faces or their actions.

G: I think listening to the news is the best way to learn English because news people speak more slowly and clearly.

Y: Unfortunately, the news doesn't give many details. It only scratches the surface. I can't learn much about my country by watching the news.

X: That's right. Seong Kim told me there was a story about a problem in Korea last night. But he said it never got to the bottom of the problem. I didn't discuss all the causes or effects.

L: I'm taking a course now on mass media—newspaper, TV, and radios. I gather from the professor's lectures and the readings that TV stories are almost never detailed. Stories are usually only 10 or 15 seconds long.

G: Really? How can TV watchers make sense of such short stories? They must be awfully hard to understand.

L: You have to read between the lines. A lot of the information comes from the pictures—not the words.

Y: Wow. You really seem to know the ins and outs of television news. How did you learn all this information, Luis?

L: My father works at a TV station in my country. That's why I'm studying it now. If I know the ropes when I return, he's promised to give me a job. But first I have to learn how TV functions.

X: Well, I think we should be out talking to people instead of watching TV.

G: That's really hard. Yesterday, I was waiting in line at the cafeteria. It seemed like an hour and I got angry. The guy behind me told me to "keep my shirt on". I had no idea what he meant. About 10 minutes later, the meaning dawned on me.

Y: What does it mean?

G: "Be patient."

L: How did you figure that out?

G: From the situation. He wasn't angry. He was calm. Besides, I don't think he was interested in my shirt!

X: That adds up. You're very good at figuring out idioms, Giovanni.

【Section 3】

Age and language learning

Most people think that the older you get, the harder it is to learn a new language. This is, they believe that children learn more easily and efficiently than adults. Thus, at some point in our lives, maybe around age 12 or 13, we lose the ability to learn languages well. Is this idea fact or myth?

Is it true that children learn a foreign language more efficiently than adults? On the contrary, research studies suggest that the opposite may be true. One report, on 2,000 Danish children studying Swedish, concluded that the teen-agers learned more, in less time, than the younger children. Another report, on Americans learning Russian, showed a direct improvement of ability over the age range tested; that is, the ability to learn increased as the age increased, from childhood to adulthood.

There are several possible explanations for these findings. For one thing, adults know more about the world and therefore are able to understand meanings more easily than children. Moreover, adults can use logical thinking to help themselves see patterns in the language. Finally, adults have more self-discipline than children.

All in all, it seems that the common idea that children are better language learners than adults may not be fact, but myth.

【Sectio 4】

Functions of intonation (3)

1. Mrs Newell has gone to see the doctor and is discussing her problem with him.

(N for Mrs Neweel, D for doctor)

D: Where is the pain, Mrs Newell?

N: Here, Doctor, in my chest.

D: I see. Here?

N: Yes, Doctor.

D: Does it hurt when you cough?

N: Yes, it does.

D: How long have you had it?

N: Six or seven weeks? As long as that?

N: I think so.

D: Have you tried taking anything—for the cough, I mean?

N: Well—the usual honey and hot lemon. And then I bought some cough syrup.

D: Did it help?

N: No, Doctor. That's why I've come to see you.

2. Jack Marsden has arranged to see his bank manager because he wants to borrow enough money to start buying a flat.

(J for Jack, B for his bank manager)

B: So, you're interested in some sort of loan, Mr Marsden?

J: That's right. You see, I want to raise enough money for a deposit on a small flat.

B: Do you mean to buy?

J: Yes. I don't want to go on renting.

B: I see. Do you think you can get a mortgage?

J: Yes. I've seen about that. You see, I've got a secure job with a good salary.

B: Is the flat for yourself? Will you be living there alone?

J: Yes. For the moment anyway. Why? Does that make any difference to the loan?

B: No, no. Just interested. That's all.

J: Do you need to know anything else? I've brought my contract with details of my salary.

B: Good. Yes, fine. And have you any securities? Shares in any companies? Insurance policies? Things like that?

Unit 18

【Section 1】

Handling an emergency

A swimming instructor is demonstrating artificial respiration for two students. Put the pictures in the correct order by writing the number in the box in each picture. Then complete the sentences underneath the pictures.

(I for Instructor, R for Ron, P for Peggy)

I: Now, once you've got the person out of the water, (mm-hmm...) the first thing you do is to get the person lying face up and check for breathing.

R: How do we do that?

I: Just listen at the mouth and nose. (Oh.) Now, if the person isn't breathing, that's probably because the airway is blocked. (Ugh!) Often with drowning victims the tongue has fallen to the back of the throat. (Ooh!) So, what you do is lift the neck from behind with one hand (Mm-hmm...) and press down on the forehead with the other; that way the head is tilted backward and the chin points upward. (Oh yeah.)

P: You mean like this?

I: Mm-hmm, yeah, that's it. (Mm, good.) Now, this should lift the tongue forward and clear the airway. OK? (Mm-hmm.) (Mm-hmm.) (MM-hmm.) If the person still isn't breathing, you've got to start artificial respiration right away. Now, watch. You're going to pinch the nostrils and at the same time keep pressure on the forehead with the same hand.

R: Hmm, it's kind of awkward with just one hand.

I: N... well, use your thumb and forefinger to pinch the nostrils (Ah.) and press with the other three fingers and the palm of your hand on the forehead — (Oh, yeah, like that.) 'cause you need the other hand to keep the neck up. (Mm-hmm.) OK?

(Mm-hmm.) Press a little harder, Peggy. (Oh, OK.) There, that's not bad. So, now, open your mouth wide, take a deep breath, and put your mouth over the victim's mouth, and blow.

R: Should we like...like seal off his mouth?

I: Yes. That's important. Thanks, Ron. Make a tight seal over the mouth. Now, the first four breaths should be given as quickly as possible. You want to get a lot of oxygen into the blood, and you want to get it in fast. (Mm-hmm.) Now, after four quick breaths, if air is getting into the lungs...

P: Yeah, but how can we...how can we tell if the air is getting into the lungs?

I: Well, you listen at the mouth and you look to see if the chest is rising. (Mm-hmm.)

P: What if it isn't?

I: Well, then you have to start again with the quick breaths. (Mm.) OK? (OK.) Any more questions?

R: No.

I: OK, so, if the air is getting into the lungs, (Mm-hmm...) continue breathing one full breath every five seconds. That's your normal rate of breathing, by the way.

R: Oh, I didn't know that.

I: Yeah, and after each breath, raise your mouth away from the face to let the air escape, (Ah.) listen for air coming out of the lungs, and look to see if the chest is falling. OK? Now, let's see you guys do it. Remember the head-tilt and neck-lift position. (Oh yeah.) That's the key. You've got to deep the head back and the chin up. Keep a steady rhythm, Peggy, (Got it.) once every five seconds. Come on, Ron, keep your finger on the nostrils (Oh yeah.)...

【Section 2】

Marriage guidance council

David and Barbara Weiner have been married for nearly fifteen years. They have two children, Gary, aged eleven, and Debbie, who is nine. During the last couple of years David and Barbara haven't been very happy. They argue all the time. Barbara's sister advised them to go to a marriage Counselor. A marriage counselor helps married couples to talk about their problems and to solve them, if possible. Sometimes they meet the counselor separately, and other times they are together for the session. This is David and Barbara's third session with Dr Joyce Sisters, the counselor.

Barbara's interview

(D for David, B for Barbara, S for Dr Joyce Sisters)

S: Oh, come in, Barbara. Have a seat. Didn't David come?

B: Yes, he's waiting outside. He didn't want to come here this week, but...well, I persuaded him to come.

S: I see. How have things been going?

B: Oh, about the same. We still seem to have fights all the time.

S: What do you fight about?

B: What don't we fight about? Oh, everything. You see, he's so inconsiderate...

S: Go on.

B: Well, I'll give you an example. You know, when the children started school, I wanted to go back to work again. So I got a job. Well, anyway, by the time I've picked Gary and Debbie up at school, I only get home about half an hour before David.

S: Yes?

B: Well, when he gets home, he expects me to run around and get dinner on the table. He never does anything in the house.

S: Hmm.

B: And last Friday! He invited three of his friends to come over for a drink. He didn't tell me to expect them, and I'd had a long hard day. I don't think that's right, do you?

S: Barbara, I'm not here to pass judgement. I'm here to listen.

B: I'm sorry. And he's so messy. He's worse than the kids. I always have to remind him to pick up his clothes. He just throws them on the floor. After all, I'm not his maid. I have my own career. Actually, I think that's part of the trouble. You see, I make more money than he does.

S: David! I'm so glad you could come.

D: Hello, Dr Sisters. Well, I'll be honest. Barbara had to force me to come, really.

S: Does it embarrass you to talk about your problems?

D: Sure, it does. But I guess we need to talk to somebody.

S: Barbara feels that you...well, that you resent her job.

D: I don't know. I'd like her to stay home, but she's very smart. So really, I encouraged her to go back to work. With the kids in school, she need something to do. And I suppose we need the money.

S: How do you share the house work?

D: I try to help. I always help her with the dishes, and I help Gary and Debbie to do their homework while she makes dinner. But she doesn't think that's enough. What do you think?

S: I'm not here to give an opinion, David.

D: I think we're both too tired, that's all. In the evenings we're both too tired to talk. And Barbara... she never allows me to suggest anything about the house or about the kids. We always have the same arguments. She has her own opinions and that's it. Last night we had another fight. She's forbidden the kids to ride their bikes to school.

S: Why?

D: She thinks they're too young to ride in the traffic. But I think they should. She always complains about picking them up at school. But they can't be tied to their mother's apron strings all their lives, can they?

【Section 3】

Pronunciation achievement factors

We all know that it is difficult for adults to learn accurate pronunciation in a foreign language. We also know that some people achieve better results than others. Why is this? What are the factors that might predict which students will achieve good pronunciation? If we knew the factors helping pronunciation, we could improve our own language.

Richard Suter, a language researcher at a California university, decided to test the relative importance of factors that might predict which students would achieve the most accurate pronunciation. He wanted to find out if there are any factors a student could change in order to improve performance.

The first thing Suter did was to make a list of all the factors that might possibly show which students would learn the best pronunciation. Then he compared these factors with the pronunciation of a group of foreign students. Here is a list of six of the factors that Suter studied.

1. Sex. Do females learn better than males?

2. Mother tongue. Is it easier to learn a language close to one's own?

3. Personality. Do out-going people learn pronunciation better than shy people?

4. Attitude toward pronunciation. Does it make a difference if the student believes that pronunciation is a very important part of language?

5. Natural ability. How important is the ability to mimic, or imitate? Most people assume that natural ability is the single most important factor in learning pronunciation.

6. Conversation with natives. Does the amount of conversation in English, with native speakers of English, make a significant difference?

When Suter compared the students' pronunciation accuracy scores with these six variables, some of the results were surprising. He found that two of the factors did not have any relation to the accuracy of pronunciation. That is, these two factors were not at all significant in predicting who would do well learning pronunciation. These two factors were:

1. Sex. Females were not better than males.

2. Personality. Out-going people were not better at pronuncia-

tion than shy people.

Suter concluded from these results that the factors of sex and personality were not significant predictors of pronunciation accuracy. On the other hand, he found that four variables did make a significant difference. I will give them to you in order of importance. That is, the most important predictors come first.

1. Mother tongue. This was the most significant factor in predicting achievement. If the student's own language was closer to English, the achievement was likely to be greater.

2. Attitude about pronunciation. This was the second most important factor in predicting achievement. In fact, a belief in the importance of pronunciation was far more important than any of the remaining factors. After the mother tongue factor, this factor of attitude was the single most significant variable in predicting good pronunciation learning.

3. Conversation with natives. Third most important variable. The ability to imitate helped, but it was not nearly as significant as most people think. It was far less significant than the first three.

Suter concluded that the three most significant predictors in achievement in pronunciation are: 1) the student's mother tongue, 2) the belief in the importance of pronunciation, and 3) the amount of time spent in conversations with native speakers.

The conclusions of this research are encouraging. Of course, we can't change factor 1, our mother tongue. But we do have control over factors 2 and 3, which are the next most important variables in learning accurate pronunciation. First, we can decide that pronunciation is important, and second, we choose to make the effort to speak the new language with natives. You might say that our own choice is the most significant factor in achievement in the new language.

【Section 4】

Thought group (1)

Part 2

2. (1) $(2+3)\times 5=55$ (2) $2+(3\times 5)=17$
   (3) $3\times(3+5)=24$ (4) $(3\times 3)+5=14$
   (5) $(3-2)\times 6=6$ (6) $(4-2)\times 5=10$
   (7) $4-(2\times 5)=-6$ (8) $(6\div 2)+5=15$
   (9) $(16\div 4)\times 2=8$ (10) $16-(4\times 2)=8$
3. telephone numbers. Make sure you group the mumbers together correctly.

   Patrick's number: 93 98 20 58

   The radio station's number: 19 39 184 29 09 34

Unit 19

【Section 1】

Apartment hunting

A man phones a building superintendent for information about an apartment for rent. Fill in the answers to his questions on the checklist.

(B for Mrs Benevento, J for Jim)

B: Hello?

J: Hi. Um... I'm calling about... uh... the apartment that was advertised in the Gazette? Is that still available?

B: Yes, it is.

J: Now, that's a two-bedroom?

B: That's right. It's two bedrooms, a kitchen, a living room, and the living room can also be used as a dining room.

J: Uh-huh. Uh, what's the rent on that?

B: It's four hundred and twenty-five dollars a month.

J: Uh, does that include heat and electricity?

B: No. The tenants have to pay their own utilities.

J: Huh. Uh, what's... uh... the average cost of utilities, do you know?

B: Oh, I guess between thirty-five and forty dollars a month.

J: Mm-hmm. Uh... do you have... uh... washers and dryers in the building?

B: Well, yes. There's a laundry room. It has three washers and dryers.

J: Uh-huh. That's good. Where we live now is... it's really noisy. I... is this like a fairly quiet building?

B: Oh, yes! Well, the neighbors are really considerate, and no pets are allowed.

J: Oh, that's good. What floor is the apartment on?

B: Well, it's on the second floor, but there's no elevator. But it's... it's all right. I live on the third floor and I don't mind the stairs. Look, why don't you just come down and see for yourself?

J: Yeah, I'd like to see it, uh...what's the address?

B: Forty-four Turner Drive. North side of Highland Boulevard.

J: Is that close, uh, to Highland Shopping Center?

B: Oh, yes. We're only a ten-minute walk away, just a couple of minutes by car.

J: Oh, that's great, because I shop there all the time.

B: Yeah. Well, look...look, it's really a nice apartment. It's got wall-to-wall carpeting and a balcony.

J: It sounds good.

B: Well, why don't you drop by this afternoon? Ring the bell for apartment thirty-one. I'll come down and get you. Oh, and...and bring fifty dollars for a deposit, just in case you decide you want it.

J: All right, um...can I see you around...uh...five-thirty then?

B: Sure. What's your name?

J: Jim Cook. And what's yours?

B: Mary Benevento. B-E-N-E-V-E-N-T-O.

J: All right, Mrs Benevento, um...I'll see you later...um...bye.

B: Bye.

【Section 2】

Out of work

In the United States a lot of people are out of work. Tracy Kowalski is 19. She dropped out of high school two years ago and got a job as a check-out clerk in a supermarket. She was fired four months ago and hasn't been able to find another job yet.

"My old man just doesn't understand. He started working in the steel mill here in town when he was 16. Things are different now, but he thinks I should start bringing home some money. I'm on unemployment, but it isn't very much and I'm just fed up with standing in line to sign for it every other week. I hate having to ask my folks for money. My mom gives me a couple of dollars now and then. But she can't stand having me around the house all day. I've almost given up looking for a job. I look at the paper every day, but I'm really tired of going through the want ads. There are at least fifty people for every job. I was interested in becoming a receptionist for a dentist or a doctor because I like meeting people, but now I'd take any job that came along. People ask me why I don't move to California or maybe Houston, but I really don't want to leave my family and my friends. Anyway, I'd be scared of living all alone in a strange place."

George Hartman is 54. Until last year he was a foreman at an automobile plant in Michigan. He had worked for the same company since he graduated from high school. He had a good job and a comfortable life. When the company cut back production last year, George was laid off.

"It's funny, you know. I don't feel old, but it isn't easy to start looking for a job at my age. I've been turned down so many times that now I'm afraid of applying for a job. All the interviewers are twenty years younger than me. You see, I'm interested in learning a new skill, but nobody wants to train me. I can see their point of view, you know. I'll have to retire in a few years. It's just that...well, I'm tired of sitting around the house. I've worked hard for over thirty-five years, and now I'm terrified of having nothing to do. When I was still with US Motors I was bored with doing the same thing day after day, but now I'd enjoy having a job again—any job. It's not just the money. I'm still on unemployment, and my wife has a good job. She makes more money than I ever did, but we have to be careful with expenses, and so I've given up smoking. But we're getting along. No, it's not just the money. I need to get out more and fee... useful, you know. Yeah, I guess I want to feel useful."

【Section 3】

Thought group markers

Today I want to tell you about some useful research on the way English speakers help their listeners. You know that a lot of English sentences are very complicated. The listener can get confused if the thought groups aren't clearly divided. If the groups aren't clear, the ideas wont' be clear. Each language has special ways to mark thought groups, but in English the chief marker is intonation. A researcher named O'Malley thought of a clever way to study these markers. He knew that algebra problems have to be written with parentheses. These punctuation markers are used to group the terms. If the algebra is spoken out loud, a native speaker of English can hear the grouping. Let me give you an example. Write down this equation:

$$A + (B \times C) = Y$$

Now write down another one:

$(A + B) \times C = Y$

Did you write them differently? You should have put the parentheses in different places, because these equations are different.

Perhaps you can get the idea better if I use examples from arithmetic. Write down this problem:

$2 + (3 \times 4) = 14$

Now write:

$(2 + 3) \times 4 = 20$

Did you put the parentheses in different places? The terms are exactly the same, but the grouping is different. That is why the answers are different.

The same concept of grouping also applies to words. Here's an example:

"John," said the boss, "is stupid."

That has a very different meaning form this sentence, using the same words:

John said, "The boss is stupid."

The meaning is different, just as in algebra or arithmetic. So grouping is important. Of course, speaking isn't like writing. We don't use parentheses or other punctuation when we're speaking. In fact, punctuation was invented to try to show some of the things we do in speech to separate groups of words. Written language substitutes punctuation for the spoken signals of intonation. The English listener depends on these intonation signals in order to understand clearly.

In this research on the subject of though-group markers, O'Malley tape-recorded native English speakers reading algebraic equations aloud. Then he asked some other English speakers to listen to the recordings and decide where the parentheses were placed. O'Malley found that both the speakers and listeners were very consistent in grouping the terms. The listeners were able to identify the placement of the parentheses because the speakers used two markers to show the end of a group.

The first marker was silence. That is, the speaker paused after the group, to make clear that it was finished. Listen to the pause when I read this equation:

A ... + (B × C) ... = Y

Marker 1, a pause, is quite powerful in slow speech. But in more rapid speech, there isn't time for many pauses. So the speaker has to rely on another method to mark the end of a group. Marker 2 is a change of pitch. Usually the voice pitch drops low at the end of a group. Generally, a high pitch means a new idea, and a low pitch means the end of an idea. Listen for the pitch change when I read this equation:

(A + B) × C = Y

Other researchers have confirmed these findings for spoken English. In both algebraic formulas and spoken English, the thought groups are divided by the same two markers. With Marker 1, which is especially used for slow speech, the speaker pauses at the end of each group. With Marker 2, the voice falls at the end of a group. For special clarity, both markers are used.

I've reviewed some of this research because it shows a very important way to help our listeners understand us easily. It demonstrates the ways of making thought groups clear. Clear thought groups are part of clear speech.

【Section 4】

Thought group (2)

Part 2

1. Each language has special ways to mark thought groups, but in English the chief marker is intonation.
2. (1) The listener can get confused.
   (2) You know that a lot of English sentences are very complicated.
   (3) Today I want to tell you about some useful research.
4. (1) He was shot several times.
   (2) He was shot several times to close range.
   (3) He was shot several times at close range and died shortly afterwards.
   (4) The murder took place yesterday evening when Mr Palme was walking through the streets of central Stockholm with his wife.
   (5) The gunman, who has not yet been identified.

News bulletin

The Swedish Prime Minister, Mr Olof Palme, has been assassinated. He was shot several times at close range and died shortly afterwards. The murder took place yesterday evening when Mr Palme was walking through the streets of central Stockholm with his wife, after a visit to the cinema. The gunman, who has not yet been identified, escaped in the crowd.

Mrs Thatcher will be making a full statement to the Commons this afternoon. This morning she gave her first reaction to the news describing the murder as barbaric, vicious and terrible. "I shall miss Olof Palme very deeply," she said.

Now the other news. A policeman has died after a shooting incident in the center of Manchester. Another was wounded. The gunmen escaped in a car, which it is understood has now been found abandoned.

The two sides in the ferry dispute have arrived at the London offices of the conciliation service ACAS for another attempt to end the strike.

There have been more anti-government protests in the Nigerian capital, Lagos. Twenty-eight people were injured, including fifteen policemen.

Dictation(The last news item)

The Norwegian government has arrested three members of Greenpeace, the international environmental organization. The captain and two crew members of the Greenpeace ship were escorted ashore after an incident involving damage to a Norwegian whaling vessel off the coast of northern Norway. ITC radio news.

5. (D for Diana, C for Chris)

D: Oh, Chris, it's about the visitor...

C: Yes? (adding something else)

D: They're coming on Thursday.

C: Right. (finished)

D: They should get here in the afternoon...

C: Yes? (adding something else)

D: At about 3:30.

C: Right. (finished) Who exactly is coming?

D: Well, There's Mr Nakashi and Mr Misoko...

C: Yes? (adding something else)

D: And Miss Lin.

C: Right. (finished)

D: They're staying at the Hotel Concordia...

C: Yes? (adding something else)

D: It's not a particularly nice hotel...

C: Yes? (adding something else)

D: But it's all we could get at such short notice.

C: Right. (finished)

D: So, anyway, I'll pick them up at the airport on Thursday.

C: Right. (finished)

6. (T for Training Manager, I for Interviewer)

T: And of course we're in constant touch with them by telephone.

I: Yes, tell me, er, some of the sorts of problems that you, er, get and that would call for a visit from THQ.

T: Er, well, one of the problems would be where we discover that something has gone wrong...

7. (1) "Good. How many, er, visits to school would you make."

(2) "It is difficult to say."

(3) "... and sometimes we find that we're out of the office, er, for two or three days every week."

(4) "... and then there may be a period when we're in the office for perhaps two or three weeks at a time without going outside of London other than for perhaps the odd meeting within the THQ department in London."

Unit 20

【Section 1】

Holiday plans

A: Good afternoon, madam. How can I help you?

B: Well, I want to go to Barbdos, for two weeks with a girl friend, and I was hoping you could arrange the holiday for me.

A: Yes, certainly. If you just wait a moment I'll get a booking form.

B: Thank you.

A: And we can fill it in. Here we are. Right, now have you seen a brochure?

B: Yes.

A: Do you know the holiday reference number?

B: Yes, yes, I do. Yes, the number's S151.

A: S151.

B: 02.

A: Fine, and what date would you like to leave on?

B: Oh, hopefully the 18th of January.

A: Right.

B: Yes, it's a Saturday.

A: Ah, right, it'll make a difference. And how long would you like to go for?

B: Fourteen nights.

A: Right. Could I just have your name?

B: Yes, Jameson. J A M E S O N.

A: Jameson. And the initial?

B: P.

A: Is that Mrs or Miss?

B: Miss.

A: And there are two of you?

B: Yes. My friend and I.

A: Right. Fine, and the destination is Barbados.

B: Yes, please.

A: right. Barbados. Now, would you like to stay in a hotel, an apartment, or a villa?

B: Oh, a hotel.

A: right. Do you know which hotel?

B: Yes, the Treasure Beach.

A: I've heard that's very nice.

B: Oh, good.

A: Right, now, we have three different classes of room there. There's the "standard" room, "superior" room, or what we call a "deluxe" room.

B: Oh, do you recommend any in particular?

A: Well, deluxe is rather expensive. Actually, I would take a superior, I feel for what, for the money, I think the superior is the best deal.

B: Right. Sort of middle range.

A: Yes.

B: Yes, all right. Thank you.

A: Superior, so superior. Now would that be a double or a twin?

B: A twin.

A: Right, twin superior room. I'm afraid there will be a supplement for that. We'll go through that later on.

B: Right.

A: Now, will you require bed and breakfast, half board or full board?

B: Half board, please.

A: Right. Now I think that's all I need to know. We'll just run through the cost now.

B: Yes.

A: Right.

B: How much is it for each adult?

A: Now, for that hotel at that time of the year, it'll be (1,077 per person. Now there are a few supplements I'm afraid.

B: Yes.

A: The date you want to leave is a Saturday and there'll be a (33 per person supplement for that.

B: Right, can I just write that down?

A: Yes, that's 33 for the Saturday departure.

B: Yes. That's per person?

A: Per person, yes. For the superior twin there is a 50 per person supplement.

B: Yes. Right.

A: And then for the half board it's another 235 per person. The cost is just for the room, that's stated in the brochure.

B: I see, yes, 235.

A: 235, yes.

B: Is that each?

A: That's each, yes.

B: Right.

A: So if we add all that up it comes to... let's see... 2, 790. That's the total price.

B: OK.

A: And we can guarantee it won't be any more than that.

B: I hope not!

【Section 2】

The driving test

(B for Bob, J for Jill)

B: Well? Did you?

J: No.

B: Oh no! That's the fourth time! What went wrong?

J: Everything. I didn't do a thing right. Not in the test, anyway. In the lesson before, I did it all perfectly- three-point turn emergency stop, moving off on a hill, great. The instructor said if I drove like that in the test, I'd pass.

B: So what happened?

J: Oh it's the usual thing. I just get so nervous. And the examiner was horrible. He really put me off, right from the start.

B: How? what did he do?

J: Well, he was so rude and sarcastic, so I was shaking like a leaf before we even started. If he'd been nicer and had tried to put me at ease a bit, I'm sure I'd have felt better.

B: How was he sarcastic?

J: Just to show you how nervous I was, right, I forgot to take the handbrake off when we started...

B: ...oh, no...

J: Alright, I know. And we were going down the road, and he says "Don't you think it's about time you took the handbrake off? We seem to be moving now, and I can smell it burning."

B: (laughs)

J: Well I didn't think it was very funny.

B: Sorry.

J: I felt terrible after that. I'd made a mess of things even before we got into the car. He asked me...you know, you have to read a number plate about thirty yards away, and I don't know the names of any cars. He said "What's the number of the Mercedes Two Thousand?" or something, and I got the wrong car, and he was really impatient, "No, no, no!"

B: That's not very fair, is it?

J: Then we were going along, coming to a junction, and I slowed down too soon, so the people behind got held up. They started hooting, I stalled the car...

B: ...Oh Jill...

J: and then when I got it going again, I didn't look right before pulling out into the main road...

B: But there was nothing coming, was there?

J: No, no. But I still should have looked, shouldn't I?

B: Oh...did he say anything?

J: He didn't have too. He just slammed the brakes on, you know, his dual controls, and put his hand to his forehead, like this, you know, as though he's thinking "I wonder how long I'll stay in this job", and then signaled me to go on. Well, after that there was no point in gong on, and I said so, but he just said, "Drive us back to the centre, please, Mrs Gibson." Oh my knees were knocking, honestly.

B: I bet. Poor old you. Never mind. You'll get it, of course you will.

J: I know, but what annoys me is that I know I can do all these things, really well, but not in the actual test. That's when I mess them up. When I was reversing round a corner, and doing really well, a cyclist arrived wanting to turn into the same road. I didn't know who should wait for who, so I waited, but the cyclist waved me on, or at least, I thought he had, but when I started to move he was right in front of me, and I made him swerve. If that cyclist hadn't been there, it would have been fine. when I did the emergency stop, I skidded, and I never usually do that, I just lost control for a split second, and finally when we got back to the centre and I had to park, I got too close to another parked car-just ever so slightly touched it, you know, scraped it...

B: Oh, boy. I bet you were glad when it was over, weren't you?

J: The examiner certainly was, but he didn't show it, oh no, he just calmly filled in his form, and without looking at me at all, he was looking at the sky, he said 'I'm sorry to have to inform you, Mrs Gibson that you have failed to reach the required standard'. And he got out and walked away.

B: Oh, my love. Never mind. Next time.

J: It makes me so mad. Why do people have to be so horrible?

【Section 3】

Techniques for oral presentation

In your university work, you will be expected to give oral presentations, in the form of reports or simply in the form of answers to questions. There are several things you can do to make your oral presentations clear and easy to understand.

The essential point to realize is that speech and writing are different. If you want to be clearly understood, you can't simply read your written report aloud. The biggest difference between spoken and written language is that readers can look back over the printed words when they don't understand. In spoken language, however, listeners can't go back and check the words. They can rely only on memory. So the first principle to keep in mind when you're planning to speak in public is that you have to help the listener's memory. This means that an oral report can't have as many pieces of new information packed into the same number of words, because they will come at too fast a rate for the listener to understand.

In an oral report, the rate of delivery has to be slower. One of the best ways to help your audience is simply to speak slowly. Many people speak too fast when they speak to a group. This is a mistake, especially if you have a foreign accent, because it makes listening more difficult. Beyond the simple technique of speaking more slowly when you speak before a group, there are ways of organizing your presentation that can help the listener recognize and understand your main points.

The organization of your talk should allow enough time for the listener to think both before and after each new idea. The purpose of the time before the new information is to give the audience a chance to understand the background clearly. Knowledge of the background, or setting of the information, makes it much easier to anticipate what kind of information is coming next. If the new information occurs too early, without enough background, the listener isn't prepared to understand the new idea. So before each piece of information, the listeners should be prepared with enough background to be able to predict what's coming.

I've been describing the time for thinking before the new information. It's also important to provide time for thinking after the new information. This thinking time allows listeners to fit the idea into their general knowledge of the subject. Thinking time gives the listener a chance to make sure of the idea was understood before going on to the next new idea.

There are three common ways to give the listener time for thinking after a point of new information. One way is simply to pause. A moment of silence gives the listener time to take in the new information, but there are other ways. A second method is to use a paraphrase. That is, you say the same thing, but in different words. This paraphrase, or repetition of the idea, helps the listeners to fix the thought in their memory. A third way to give the listener time to think is to use words that don't mean much. These are words that convey no information, but just fill time. For instance, you might say something like "as I've been saying" or "and so forth and so on." That kind of expression doesn't really say anything. It's just make of what we call "filler words." The words have no real meaning, but they do perform a useful function, since they allow the listener time to think.

In summary, then, we know that oral language should deliver information at a slower rate than you can use in written language. New information should be presented more gradually. Thinking time should be provided both before and after each important new item. The time before is to provide a background so that the listeners can have a chance to anticipate the idea. The time after is to allow the listeners a chance to understand what they just heard. The three most common ways to allow this thinking time are: 1) to pause, 2) to paraphrase, and 3) to use filler words.

I hope that these suggestions will help make your oral presentations a great success.

【Section 4】

Listening for positive results

Part 2

Listening involves much more than hearing. People's physical ability to hear is generally excellent and if a disability affects hearing, mechanical aids are available. Hearing is only the first step in the listening process. Once received, the message must be interpreted. Interpretation is a mental, not a physical, process. A final step is for the receiver to determine what action should be taken. The message might be stored for later use, as is done with educationally learned material, or it might be dismissed as is often done with insignificant messages.

We listen to (1) receive information, (2) solve problems, (3) share with others, and (4) persuade or dissuade. Each reason may call for a different style of listening or for a combination of styles.

Generally speaking, one can put the daily listening activities into two categories: intensive listening and casual listening.

Intensive Listening

When we listen to obtain information, solve problems, or persuade or dissuade (as in arguments), we listen intensively . Intensive listening requires that we marshal all our listening forces to be successful. Intensive listening can be achieved by following some of these suggestions:

1. Try to become involved in the material by making written or mental notes.

2. Attempt to predict or anticipate the speaker's future points.

3. Watch speakers for any nonverbal clues that will help you understand the speaker's point of view and emotional state.

4. Provide listener with feedback either orally or through nonverbal nods, facial expressions, or body movements to encourage further speaker comments and behavior adjustment.

5. Try to avoid yielding to your stereotypes, personal judgments, and distractions.

Casual Listening

Listening for pleasure, recreation, amusement, and relaxation is casual listening. Some people have the radio on all day long; it provides background music and talk during daily routines and work periods, just as the car radio provides "companionship" for most commuters. Casual listening provides relaxing "breaks" for more serious tasks and supports ours emotional health.

An interesting concept about all listening, but particularly true of casual listening, is that people are selective listeners. We listen to what we want. In a crowded room in which everyone seems to be talking, you can block out all the noise and engage in the conversation you are having with someone.

Casual listening doesn't require much emotional or physical effort, which is one of the reasons people engage in "small talk" and "chitchat".

News Item

A Jordanian diplomat has been shot in Beirut in what has been viewed as a political killing. The embassy's first-secretary was attacked as he drove out of the parking-lot near his home.

Key

Unit 1

【Section 1】

Task

(1) 466	(2) 572	(3) 761	(4) 829	(5) 653
(6) 275	(7) 187	(8) 593	(9) 960	(10) 640
(11) 360	(12) 330	(13) 316	(14) 814	(15) 218
(16) 113	(17) 302	(18) 408	(19) 601	(20) 804
(21) 203	(22) 503	(23) 106	(24) 409	(25) 457
(26) 321	(27) 515	(28) 392	(29) 519	(30) 919
(31) 698	(32) 481	(33) 728	(34) 777	(35) 820
(36) 104	(37) 419	(38) 886	(39) 559	(40) 632

【Section 3】

Task 1

(1) Canada (2) Atlantic Ocean (3) Mexico (3) Pacific Ocean

Task 2

(1) 3,600,000 square miles

(2) the Appalachian Mountains; the Rocky Mountains

(3) the Ohio; the Missouri; the Mississippi

【Section 4】

Part 2

1. (1) three problems

(2) identifying, remembering, following the argument

(3) Because it is hard to separates the words from each other in speech and some words have a weak form.

(4) identifying the words correctly, understanding by the meaning, remembering what has been said, following the argument

2. (1) F (2) T (3) F (4) F (5) T

Unit 2

【Section 1】

Task 1

(1) 5,896 (2) 7,906 (3) 4,494 (4) 5,515
(5) 26,960 (6) 75,682 (7) 28,657 (8) 38,024
(9) 57,490 (10) 63,818 (11) 99,233 (12) 16,997
(13) 621,844 (14) 392,835 (15) 302,798
(16) 275,390 (17) 879,930 (18) 911,909
(19) 719,056 (20) 104,308
(21) 6,752,431 (22) 9,879,041 (23) 8,100,003
(24) 5,663,174 (25) 3,312,765 (26) 2,007,009
(27) 4,276,390 (28) 1,060,030 (29) 12,456,800
(30) 50,060,120 (31) 44,731,556 (32) 68,238,730
(33) 140,732,55 (34) 164,504,832 (35) 193,116,583
(36) 150,040,070 (37) 647,325,360 (38) 730,004,015
(39) 343,506,104 (40) 975,075,055

Task 2

① 30,000 ② 45 ③ 13 ④ 1929 ⑤ 1953 ⑥ 14

⑦ 1975 ⑧ $ 24,500 ⑨ 18 ⑩ $ 750 ⑪ 1976 ⑫ 15
⑬ $ 300,000 ⑭ 1982 ⑮ $ 7,000,000 ⑯ 150 ⑰ 7,000

【Section 3】

Task 2

① New York ② Ohio ③ Indiana ④ Illinois ⑤ Iowa
⑥ Nebraska ⑦ Virginia ⑧ Thomas Jefferson ⑨ third
⑩ 4,200 ⑪560 ⑫ Washington ⑬ California ⑭ Oregon
⑮ natural resources ⑯ fishing ⑰ oil ⑱ 3,200 ⑲ the Pacific ⑳ California

【Section 4】 Listen Efficiently

Part 3

① good byes ② understand ③ cold ④ get out of here
⑤ go on ⑥ watch ⑦ here ⑧ this night ⑨ my body
⑩ the best thing ⑪ thankful ⑫ thankful ⑬ honor
⑭ survive ⑮ give up ⑯ hopeless ⑰ let go of that
⑱ promise ⑲ let go ⑳ never let go ⑳ never let go
㉑ never let go

Unit 3

【Section 1】

Task 1

(1) Jameson (2) Juliet Henderson (3) Stephen
(4) Loughborough (5) Gerald Leary (6) Mahoney

(7) Bailey (8) Greenwich (9) Seabourne

(10) Gloucester

Task 2

(1) (649)545-4867 (2) (8610)6647-8219

(3) (141)6945-1816 (4) (612)4546-8016

(5) (309)822-5920 (6) (670)266-3315

Task 3

(1)

John Mitchell
15 Brougham Place
OXFORD
Tel 223-6790

(2)

Joe Harding
The Manhattan Building
2563 Orchard Road
SINGAPORE
Tel 236 47539

【Section 2】

	Information	
Name of guest(s)	Paul Smith	
Number of guests	1	
No. of nights	1	
Room type	□ Executive ✓ □ twin □ smoking	✓ □ Standard □ double-bedded ✓ □ non-smoking
Address	5383 Collins Avenue, Miami Zip code: 23892	
Method of payment	Visa card	
Reserved	□ Yes	✓ □ No

【Section 3】

Task 1

① four ② elementary school ③ junior high school ④ senior

high school ⑤ college ⑥ a drama club ⑦ a foreign language club ⑧ a photography club ⑨ basketball ⑩ football ⑪ baseball ⑫ track

Task 2

(1) F (2) F (3) T

【Section 4】

Part 2

1. ① sound ② language ③ adults ④ native ⑤ lose ⑥ spelling rules ⑦ real sound ⑧ about ⑨ misconceptions ⑩ hear
2. ① fast ② run ③ opposite ④ quickly ⑤ strong intonation ⑥ easily ⑦ simultaneously ⑧ appearance ⑨ sound ⑩ conversational ⑪ smooth ⑫ fluid ⑬ word by word ⑭ sounding mechanical ⑮ foreign ⑯ sound group ⑰ sound units ⑱ smoothly ⑲ flowing along
3. ① intonation ② liaisons ③ pronunciation ④ systematic ⑤ structural ⑥ free form ⑦ intuitive ⑧ creative ⑨ what you mean ⑩ how you mean it ⑪ tone ⑫ feeling

Unit 4

【Section 1】

Part 1

(1) 1:59

(2) 6:15

(3) 9:30

(4) 5:05

(5) ① 3:40 ② 5:05 ③ 7:55 ④ 11:00

(6) ① 4:30 ② 6:45 ③ 8:30 ④ 10:45

Task 2

	Dates and times	Events
(1)	August 3rd, 9:30 am	Dental appointment
(2)	July 28th, 8 pm	Cindy's party
(3)	August 10th, 11:15 am	Aunt arrives
(4)	July 26th, 3 pm	Tennis game
(5)	September 22nd, 6 pm	Meet Francis
(6)	August 2nd, 2 pm	Trip date

【Section 2】

Task 1 C-B-E-D-F-A

Task 2

(1) No, he finished work in the evening.

(2) No, he was hot.

(3) Yes, it started to rain heavily.

(4) No, he saw a young girl.

(5) Yes, she was.

(6) Yes, he did.

(7) No, she didn't.

(8) Yes, he did.

(9) Yes, she was.

(10) No, she wasn't.

(11) No, he didn't.

【Section 3】

Task 1

① Community colleges ② colleges and universities ③ graduate programs ④ automobile repair ⑤ electricity ⑥ photography ⑦ graduate programs ⑧ advanced study

Task 2

(1) F (2) T (3) F (4) F

【Section 4】

Part 2

1. (1) "I think, first of all, we ought, to ask him." 10 words

   (2) "Is he busy on Monday evening?" 6 words

2. ① were riding ② from around ③ us or ④ was a ⑤ sped directly ⑥ past us ⑦ our ⑧ than an inch ⑨ Was any one else around ⑩ And ⑪ never even ⑫ even know ⑬ run a ⑭ Wonder if ⑮ anyone else ⑯ me a bit ⑰ What was ⑱ Did something ⑲ Not that ⑳ just happened to ㉑ not the first time ㉒ happened ㉓ That doesn't sound like ㉔ just wish ㉕ on me

Unit 5

【Section 1】

Task 1

NAME OF COINS	TOTAL CENTS
2 nickels	10
3 dimes	30
2 pennies and 2 quarters	52
3 dimes and 1 quarter	55
1 dime, 2 nickels and 1 quarter	45

Task 2

	Total	Change
(1)	$ 10.00	$ 10.00
(2)	$ 19.90	$ 0.10
(3)	$ 9.65	$ 7.35
(4)	$ 8.15	$ 11.52
(5)	$ 12.49	$ 5.51
(6)	$ 18.25	$ 1.75

【Section 2】

Task 1 B-D-E-A-C-H-G-F

Task 2

(1) driving through

(2) an old film star

(3) butler

(4) She lives with her memories of reading letters which she believes are from her fans, but which her butler writes.

(5) a young writer

(6) kills him

【Section 3】

Task 1

① Thomas Jefferson

② the independence of the 13 original colonies from Great Britain

③ reasons for the separation ④ the principles for which the Revolutionary War was fought ⑤ Philadelphia ⑥ 1787

⑦ Maryland ⑧ Virginia

Task 2

(1) T (2) F (3) F

【Section 4】

Part 2

1. (2) A: How often do I have to do it?

B: You ought to do every exercise once a week.

A: Do I have to do every exercise?

B: Yes, it should take you about two hours. Though I don't suppose it will.

(4) A: Actually, I ought to practice more regularly I suppose.

B: Well, don't worry about it. I often forget myself.

A: Perhaps we ought to try and go together.

(5) A: How's it going, Edward.

B: Not bad at all. It's not exactly a busy place though.

A: Where are you staying?

B: Just a little pub on the edge of town.

A: And what are you doing on your own?

B: Not a lot actually. This evening there's a match on TV, so I'll get a snack in town and watch a bit of football afterwards.

2. (2) A: Can I help you, sir?

B: Yes, I'm in a rush I'm afraid. Can I have a piece of apple cake please, with ice cream ?

A: Certainly, sir. I'll ask the waiter to come over as soon as possible.

(4) A: Switch off the light, David. It's almost eleven.

B: I'm scared of the dark. I think I heard a noise. Look over there! Something on the window ledge is moving.

Unit 6

【Section 1】

Chicago: now—rain, 38 degrees F.

Tomorrow—cloudy, scattered showers 45 degrees Fahrenheit high, 32 degrees F. at night

Sunday—more rain, colder

San Francisco: showers

Los Angeles: fair weather, in the low seventies

San Diego: fair

Denver: 38 degrees F. 30-mile-an-hour wind, cold & windy weekend

Dallas: cold, 48 degrees F.

Detroit: rain, may turn to snow, 43 degrees, F.

Toronto: rain, may turn to snow, 41 degrees F.

Montreal: snow

New York: snow

Miami: clear sky, sunny, 78 degrees F.

【Section 3】

Task 1

① Federal ② the nation as a whole ③ makes ④ carries out ⑤ interprets ⑥ mint ⑦ tax ⑧ keep ⑨ a navy ⑩ an air force ⑪ conduct ⑫ local affairs ⑬ health ⑭ education ⑮ local taxes

Task 2

Three Branches of the Federal Government

the Legislative	the Executive	the Judicial
the House of Representatives the Senate Congress made up of two houses meet in the Capitol	the President lives in the White House administers the laws with his cabinet	nine judges of the Supreme Court

Task 3

(1) F (2) T

【Section 4】

Part 2

1. (1) Listen to these words and mark the linking.

Please stop pushing. He opened the big gate.

Cook it in a deep pot. He plans to rob both.

She has a black cat. That's a bad dog.

Put ten in the box. Where's the red door?

(2) Listen to the following sentences. Connect the words that are linked.

① I wish she knew.

② How come Mary was absent?

③ Let's stay late tonight.

④ Come Monday, not Tuesday.

2. (1) Listen to the following sentences. Mark the linking.

① He was sick yesterday.

② Get rid of that.

③ Meet them in the lobby.

④ I've had it with them.

⑤ Let's play it by air.

⑥ As I was saying, now's not a good time.

(2) Listen to the conversation and fill in the blanks with the words you hear:

① in the

② that brand there

③ That's a lot for

④ want one

⑤ but I hadn't planned on

⑥ that much

⑦ going on sale next week

⑧ could give

⑨ are we talking

⑩ That settles it.

3. Notice the linking in the case of the flap.

① better off ② put off ③ paid off ④ get over

⑤ out and out ⑥ head on home (on out, on over)

⑦ tired out ⑧ fed up ⑨ get caught up

⑩ get it over with ⑪ have had it with some one

⑫ might as well

4. Listen and fill in the blanks with the words you hear.

① a gentle dentist ② count on ③ went to ④ get ⑤ an

⑥ caught up on ⑦ water the plants ⑧ out a little ⑨ meant it

Unit 7

【Section 1】

Airlines	Flight Number	Departure Gate	Destination
(1) United Airlines	305	35	San Francisco
(2) Japan Airlines	29	16	Tokyo
(3) Delta Airlines	6120	23B	Los Angeles
(4) NorthWest Airlines	13	11A	Miami
(5) Cathay Pacific	300	35	Hong Kong
(6) Air France	603	19B	Paris
(7) American Airlines	55	33A	Mexico City
(8) British Airways	16	25A	London

【Section 2】

(1) shaving kit
(2) key
(3) safe pocket for the traveler's checks
(4) a book to read on the plane
(5) small change to make phone calls
(6) have someone to meet him in Los Angeles
(7) have a reservation
(8) call parents tonight

【Section 3】

Task 1

① hold ultimate power ② five ③ voting ④ 100
⑤ the ruling ⑥ Prime Minister ⑦ 651 ⑧ examine

Task 2

① Government ② Parliament ③ House of Commons
④ House of Lords ⑤ the Monarchy ⑥ MP ⑦ Opposition

【Section 4】

Part 2

1. ① Care for ② bite ③ Were ④ asking for me ⑤ I believe so ⑥ you look ⑦ helps to talk ⑧ going to do this ⑨ Probably sleep ⑩ you want to do ⑪ going to do ⑫ and chocolate ⑬ for ⑭ or ⑮ Have you ⑯ I have ⑰ from her ⑱ Have they gone ⑲ his ⑳ Have I ㉑ Have we ㉒ Has the ㉓ her ㉔ if he
2. ① or ② or ③ and ④ or ⑤ 've you been ⑥ I've

been away ⑦ I've been over ⑧ you've had ⑨ I think everything's ⑩ I've had ⑪ than I ⑫ you have any ⑬ And ⑭ have any ⑮ Has anything ⑯ I've also been having ⑰ Have you seen a ⑱ if he could do anything ⑲ worth a ⑳ one I have ㉑ you her ㉒ Give her a ㉓ You've ㉔ gotten caught up on ㉕ putting them off ㉖ end up ㉗ waiting to ㉘ certainly ㉙ I wanted to ㉚ a beating ㉛ last few months ㉜ starting to ㉝ invests at ㉞ kidding ㉟ all on her own ㊱ What do you know ㊲ getting to know

3. ① She'll be ② you ③ She's ④ and she's ⑤ her ⑥ and ⑦ they're ⑧ to ⑨ They ⑩ to ⑪ they'll be ⑫ to ⑬ if you're ⑭ after

Unit 8

【Section 1】

	Age	Height	Hair
(1)	17	about average	curly blond
(2)	about 20	about 170 centimeters	short curly
(3)	7	/	light brown
(4)	5	/	curly
(5)	10	/	long blond
(6)	in her teens	about average	short blond

【Section 2】

Task 3

① 15 ② TV ③ computer ④ phone ⑤ stricter ⑥ lonely ⑦ friends ⑧ aunts ⑨ cousins ⑩ grown-up ⑪ being an "only child"

【Section 3】

Task 1

① a hundred ② 2,000 ③ stages ④ House of Commons ⑤ the House of Lords ⑥ monarch also ⑦ Public Bills ⑧ Private Bills

Task 2

(1) T (2) T (3) F (4) F

【Section 4】

Part 2

2. (1) ① A ② A ③ B ④ A ⑤ A

(2) ① (h)e ② (h)e ③ (h)im ④ (h)im ⑤ (h)im ⑥ (h)e ⑦ (h)e

3. (1) ① p**o**lice ② secret**a**ry ③ p**e**rhaps ④ vege**t**able ⑤ **e**xcuse me ⑥ c**o**rrect ⑦ p**o**tato ⑧ Comf**or**table ⑨ **I'm a**fraid so

(2) Consonant cluster

① tex**t**books ② nex**t** week ③ three-fif**th**s ④ he mus**t** be ill ⑤ he ask**ed** Paul ⑥ she look**ed** back quickly

(3) Nonreleased final consonants

① great ② cab ③ card ④ up

(4) ① gen**e**rous ② horr**i**ble ③ Cab**i**net ④ temp**e**rature
⑤ diff**e**rent ⑥ asp**i**rin ⑦ gas**o**line ⑧ g**a**rage
⑨ reference ⑩ fav**ou**rite

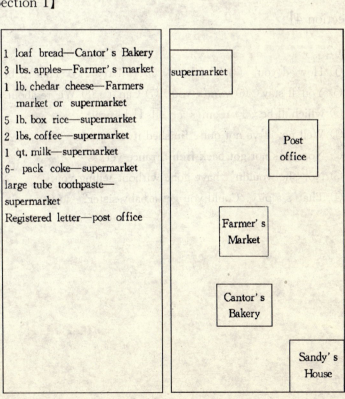

Unit 9

【Section 1】

1 loaf bread—Cantor's Bakery
3 lbs. apples—Farmer's market
1 lb. chedar cheese—Farmers market or supermarket
5 lb. box rice—supermarket
2 lbs. coffee—supermarket
1 qt. milk—supermarket
6- pack coke—supermarket
large tube toothpaste—supermarket
Registered letter—post office

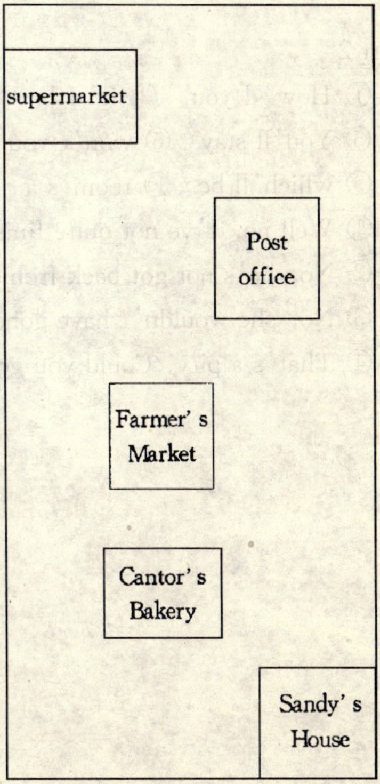

【Section 3】

Task 1

(1) F (2) T (3) T

Task 2

① support ② love ③ parental authority ④ stability ⑤ chastity ⑥ elderly ⑦ sociologists ⑧ the nuclear family ⑨ extended family ⑩ households ⑪ shrinking ⑫ crisis ⑬ social ⑭ drug taking ⑮ juvenile crime ⑯ disintegrating

【Section 4】

Part 2

1. ① How'd you ② it'd be ③ I'll try ④ That'd be ⑤ You'll stay ⑥ won't you ⑦ Can't ⑧ We're about to ⑨ which'll be ⑩ room's a ⑪ I'd say it
2. ① Well no, I've not quite finished it.
   ② No, he's not got back from France yet.
   ③ No, she wouldn't have gone without telling you.
   ④ That's a pity. Could you get a baby-sister?

Unit 10

【Section 1】

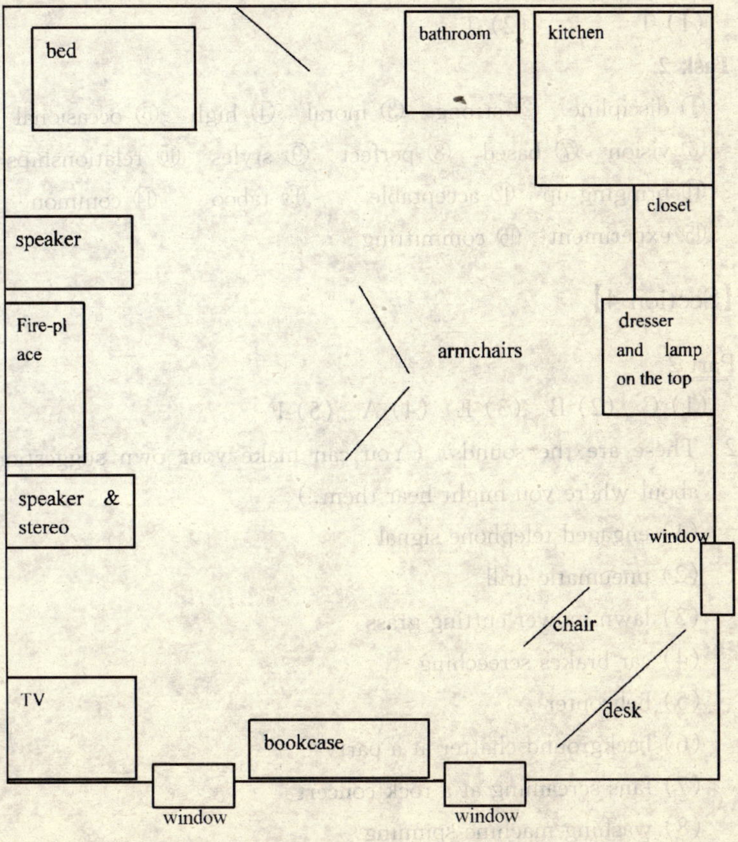

【Section 2】

Task 3

(1) I (2) E (3) B (4) J (5) G

(6) D (7) A (8) C (9) H (10) F

【Section 3】

Task 1

(1) T (2) T

Task 2

① discipline ② strong ③ moral ④ high ⑤ occasional
⑥ vision ⑦ based ⑧ perfect ⑨ styles ⑩ relationships
⑪ bringing up ⑫ acceptable ⑬ taboo ⑭ common
⑮ experiment ⑯ committing

【Section 4】

Part 2

(1) C (2) B (3) E (4) A (5) F

2. These are the sounds. (You can make your own suggestions about where you might hear them.)

(1) engaged telephone signal

(2) pneumatic drill

(3) lawn mower cutting grass

(4) car brakes screeching

(5) helicopter

(6) background chatter at a party

(7) fans screaming at a rock concert

(8) washing machine spinning

(9) glass smashing

(10) a dog barking

3.

	Speaker	Sound	Place	Situation
(1)	reporter	aircraft taking off or landing airport	possibly a strike or disruption of services	
(2)	motorist	traffic	possibly a motorway	car broken down
(3)	car owner	car alarm	possibly a car park	car owner apprehending a thief who is breaking into his car
(4)	employee at a large store	crackle and tone of a public address system	supermarket or department store	another employee is being called, possibly to help exchange goods
(5)	sports correspondent	football crowd	large football ground	important football match
(6)	dog owner	children playing	park	owner throwing a stick for the dog to run after, near a children's playground

4. (1) A protest about people being threatened with eviction from their homes because of a proposed new road.

(2) An advert for a trip in a hot air balloon.

(3) An advert for a new vacuum cleaner which can do many different jobs.

(4) A financial report about a company about to go bankrupt.

(5) An announcement saying that a short holiday in Holland will include an excursion to see the bulb[tulip]fields where the flowers are grown.

Unit 11

【Section 1】

Things to do—Aug. 29	
Call Clarkson College about computer programming courses—TODAY!	
Name of course:	Data Processing
Which evening(s)?	Monday evening
Time:	7:00—9:45
Dates: Starts—	first week in September
Ends—	twenty-first in December
Cost:	$ 300
Registration	
When:	Sep. 2nd, Sep. 3rd, 6:00—9:00pm
Where:	round building, Frost Auditorium
What to bring:	check book

【Section 2】

Task 3

(1) F (2) E (3) H (4) I (5) C

(6) A (7) J (8) G (9) B (10) D

【Section 3】

Task 1

(1) psychological, cultural and linguistic problems

(2) linguistic

(3) 4 pieces of advice

Task 2

(1) T (2) F (3) F (4) F (5) T

【Section 4】

Part 2

1. 5 syllables: administration / examination / simplification / clarification / justification

   6 syllables: identification / reinterpretation / reunification

   8 syllables: internationalization

2. computerization →he works at the station

   interruption → shocked the nation

   addition → the action

   clarification →who did she mention

   communication → another option

4. Regular syllable length

   (1) (2) (4) (6) (7) (11)

   Irregular syllable length

   (3) (5) (8) (9) (10) (12)

Unit 12

【Section 1】

Picture 3

【Section 2】

Task 3

(1) F (2) T (3) T (4) F (5) T (6) T (7) F (8) F

【Section 3】

Task 1

(1) surprising

(2) ① Every word in English has just one meaning.

② Every word in English has an exact translational equivalemt.

③ As soon as the students know the meaning of a word, they can use it correctly.

(3) observation, imitation and repetition

Task 2

(1) F (2) T (3) F (4) T (5) T

【Section 4】

Part 2

1. (1) have; coffee; cup; tea

(2) like another

(3) Thanks; lovely meal

(4) Sorry; can't come; Monday; working late

(5) never been; car rally

(6) I usually visit; parents; Tuesdays

2. ready; Not quite; Put; coat; Just; minute; Don't rush me

3.

Telephone Message From: Jane Croft To: Chris
Messages (1) Contact Mrs. Williams before 5 / Urgent (2) Need report Wednesday (3) Send invoice Accounts Department (4) Can't go meeting Friday. / too busy

4. Check the words written by you against the transcript.

5. Good evening. This; Captain; about; attempt; crash landing; Please extinguish all cigarettes; Place; tray tables; upright, locked position; Captain says: Put; head; knees Captain says: Put; head; hands

Part 3

(1) content words and structure words

(2) content words

(3) structure words

Unit 13

【Section 1】

Menu

Appetizers		
Vegetable soup	4.50	
House salad	3.75	✓
Main dishes		
Steak with fries	18.00	
Roast chicken	9.95	
Spaghetti with meat sauce	11.00	✓
Desserts		
Apple pie	3.75	
Ice cream	2.75	
Drinks		
Tea	1.50	✓
Coffee	1.50	
Soda	1.75	
Juice	2.00	

Menu

Appetizers		
Soup of the day	4.50	✓
Salad	5.00	✓
Main dishes		
Vegetarian plate	9.50	
Grilled fish with broccoli or peas	13.00	
Desserts		
Chocolate cake	3.75	
Ice cream	2.75	✓
Drinks		
Iced Tea	1.50	
Coffee	1.50	✓
Soda	1.75	
Juice	2.00	

【Section 2】

Task 3

Gurmit and **I knew each other as children. Gurmit's mother** approached **my mother** and both of them decided the marriage. We are of similar age, **have slightly different hobbies and outlooks, but** it's worked very well.

Before any couple is introduced to each other, the parents will do a fair amount of research about the general behaviour, the education background, **the family's wealth and their standing in the society.**

I think parents have had a better experience than the children. No parent wants to see their children's marriage break up. They would choose a partner for their children and once it is arranged their children **still have complete freedom to say no and can call off the arrangement either by parents or by the couple involved.**

I think love comes out of a relationship. Once a relationship starts, you have to use it to your benefit, you have to give and take and to be tolerant.

【Section 3】

Task **1**

(1) ① To decide precisely what is the purpose to read the book.

② To get an overview of the content before starting to read.

③ To ask themselves specific questions about reading and to answer them by working notes as they read.

(2) Ask questions and answer them by making notes.

(3) 2 kinds

Task 2

(1) F (2) F (3) F (4) F (5) F

【Section 4】

Part 2

1. (1) fantastic

(2) coming; party; Saturday

(3) give

(4) think; left; bedroom

3. (1) hat; kind; sun; color; white, stripes; car; which; sold

(2) new; Nothing much, you; the States; East; West; West; San Francisco

(3) holiday; study; what; Maths; English; Neither; sick of; engineering; Electronic engineering

4. (1) What; doing; came; see Peter; Peter's not here; see; is; where; Not; friendly; are; Neither; you

(2) expensive; really; I; restaurants; you; home; cook; can't; bread; Coke; awfully; isn't; like; crazy

Unit 14

【Section 1】

1. Do you ever eat fast food? √□Yes □No
2. What kind of fast food do you normally eat?
   √1. burgers √2. sandwiches √3. pizzas √4. kebabs
3. How often do you eat fast food?
   √□ every day (*Mon.-Fri.*) □ more than once a week □ less than once a week
4. What time of day do you eat fast food?
   □ in the morning in the afternoon
   √□ around midday √□ in the evening
5. Do you eat fast food as: √□ a main meal? √□ a snack between meals?

续表

6. Which of these statements about fast food do you think are true?

(*Mark the scale*: *3 = Yes*, *2 = Maybe/Not sue*, *1 = No*)

	3	2	1
It's convenient.	√		
It tastes good.		√	
It's good for you.		√	
It's an expensive way of eating.			√
It creates litter.	√		

【Section 2】

Task 1

(1) Unless we protect nature, many wonderful places, animals and plants will disappear.

(2) A. zoology—animals, the home of large numbers of wild animals, the habitat of endangered species

B. geology—the earth itself, places that have a fantastic view or a beautiful landscape

C. biology—plants

(3) Stop hunting or pollution.

Task 2

(1) Is the place authentic? Is it real?

(2) Has this place influenced other buildings in the same country or even in another country?

(3) Is this place linked with an important religion or a philosophy?

(4) Is this place a very special example of a traditional way of life, an ancient culture or civilization?

【Section 3】

Task 1

(1) Yes.

(2) ① The errorleads to a misunderstanding or a breakdown in-communication

② The error leads to ungrammatical English

③ The error concerns style and usuage.

Task 2

(1) F (2) F (3) T (4) F (5) T

【Section 4】

Part 2

1. morning; help; Williams; name; Ribble; Riddle; Riddle; Ribble; Ribble
2. one cheese sandwich; two ham rolls; one; cheese; one cheese; two ham; rolls; two; didn't; one; write; down
3. (1) B (2) A (3) B (4) A
4. (1) You didn't go?

   (2)Promoted?

   (3) In the kitchen?

   (4) Your purse?

   (5) Postponed?
5. (1) confirming

   (2) querying

   (3) querying

   (4) confirming

   (5) querying

(6) confirming

(7) querying

Unit 15

【Section 1】

About his character	Speaker 1	Speaker 2
He is very determined.	A	
He's unsure of himself.		A
He's a practical person.		A
He's an imaginative person.	A	A
About his past		
He was probably ill when he was younger.	A	
He wasn't sure what to do when he was younger.		A
About his future		
He'll continue in the same job.		A
He'll have important relationships with two women.	A	
He'll retire early.		A

【Section 2】

Task 1

Stephanie's first encounters with the spirit	The night she first saw the spirit	The night the pictures fell off the wall	The things you think going to happen next
I often had this strange feeling that I was being watched...and...I started talking to myself... in my head, not out loud, saying "Oh, don't be silly, there's nobody there, there's nothing at all." And I carried on having this feeling, so I began to talk actually out loud, saying "Now, come on, I know you're there, don't bother me." And the same would happen while I was working, I would suddenly feel that someone was there, and once I'd talked to it, it was OK.	we were lying in bed one night, and suddenly we both woke up, and there was somebody standing at the bottom of the bed, this figure, and we presumed it was John, one of the friends we were living with, who wanted something. So we said "What's the matter, what do you want?" and there was no answer... I said "It's not John, it doesn't look like John." It was this tall figure. I put the light on, and... there was nothing there...	Then a few days later, Jeremy woke me up in the middle of the night. He woke me up... it was freezing cold... each picture was falling off the wall... one by one... from left to right around the room. And when Jeremy woke me up, he was absolutely petrified...About half the pictures were on the floor, and each one dropped off one by one, all the postcards... off the board... and then the board and then the next board... And it went right round the room, until every single piece of paper was on the floor or the bed. We were sitting in bed covered in pieces of paper, absolutely terrified of what was going to happen next.	

Task 2

(2) ① Is anybody there?

② Are you a man?

③ Do you live in this house?

(3) ① man ② the house was built ③ built ④ the early nineteenth century ⑤ his room ⑥ happy ⑦ around ⑧ on his own

【Section 3】

Task 1

(1) Be good at asking questions.

(2) The teacher interprets the intended question as a comment.

(3) ① preface their questions with an introductory statements

② be careful to locate the exact point of their questions on a text

③ Employ a question form

Task 2

(1) F (2) F (3) T (4) T (5) T

【Section 4】

Part 2

1\. (1) ① He's trying to take a photograph of Louise.

② Because he wants to get everything just right: the light, the position, Louise's expression, etc.

③ Louise is very impatient and intolerant of Alan's fuss. She would prefer a snapshot approach.

(2) The words that are noticeable

Turn, towards / head / Right / slightly

(3) The words that are highlighted

Just/Right/Closer/Wall

My/Not So

Lift/Up/Like That
Right/Not Quite
Tense/How/Smile
Know/Feel/Can
Needn't Look/Natural
Exactly/beFore
Exactly

2. (1) Answers to the questions

① Samantha had told Lisa that she has received a dozen red roses from an anonymous admirer.

② John explains that the red roses mean "He's in love with her."

③ Lisa: to be pitied

John: to have less than is really necessary, *eg* money

(2) ① Phrase highlighted

a dozen roses

② Explanation

Lisa wants John to notice what and how many.

At this point John knows she got a dozen but he's not sure what.

At this point John has just mentioned roses. Now Lisa wants to emphasize how many.

(3) ① Phrase highlighted in love with

② Explanation

John is explaining that sending red roses means more than being "just keen". It means being in love, so he highlights this information.

The idea of "being in love" is not questioned here. What's

important is who is in love with whom.

3. (1) B (2) B (3) A (4) B (5) A

Unit 16

【Section 1】

Task 1

Game A	Game B	Game C	Game D
thimble	bof chocolate jacket pair of gloves dice hat scarf knife and fork	bath cap eggs towel	roll of toilet paper

【Section 2】

Task 3

(1) J (2) D (3) G (4) H (5) B

(6) A (7) I (8) E (9) F (10) C

【Section 3】

Task 1

(1) seminars and tutorials

(2) ① To help discuss and clarify difficulties students have.

② To obtain more intimate and personal contract with students.

(3) ① Speed of the dialegue is too fast.

② Students may not know how to break ints a discussion politely.

③ Students may not know how to formulate questions quickly and accurately.

Task 2

(1) F (2) F (3) F (4) T (5) T

【Section 4】

<u>Part 2</u>

1. (1) Answers to the questions

① It falls. The pitch movement begins on "give" and continues to fall through "Claire".

② "Yes. Dave does not make" Claire prominent here, which suggests that he does not need to draw attention to the word. This is usually the case when the idea expressed is already in play.

③ No. Dave presents "give" as a new idea at this point. Dave and Gill have probably mentioned Claire and the fact that it is her birthday or some special occasion but this is the point at which the idea of giving her something is introduced.

(2) Answers to the questions

① The pitch movements are: "reading" \↗, "book" ↘.

② Yes. Gill assumes that Dave knows Claire likes reading; she believes it is knowledge shared by them both at this point.

2. Answers to the questions

(1) ① Tony is worried that he has spoiled his chances of getting the job he wanted because he was not wearing suitable clothes at the interview.

② Yes. She tells Tony, "I'm sure you needn't worry", before she hears he wore jeans.

(2) ① Identification and ②explanation:

Tony: ... \↗ I MANaged to answer all the QUESTions // \↗ and I THINK I said the right THINGS // ... ↘ I wore the right CLOTHES //

Explanation: \↗ shared knowledge, ↘ unexpected by his listener

Lisa: ... // \↗ what's DONE // ↘ is DONE //

Explanation: \↗ shared knowledge, ↘ telling him sth.

Tony: ... // \↗ there's NOTHING I can DO about it // ... // \↗ I CAN'T CHANGE anything // ↘ but I CAN'T help THINKing about it //

Explanation: \↗ referring to what Lisa has just said and referring to the same thing, ↘ telling sth. he thinks she doesn't know.

Identification and explanation:

Lisa: ... // \↗ you needn't WORRY // ↘ what DID you wear // ...

Explanation: ↘ indicating that the information will be new to her.

Tony: // ↘ I HAD to put my JEANS on //

Explanation: ↘ telling her sth. new

Lisa: // \↗ Your JEANS // ...

Explanation: \↗ referring directly to what he has just said.

Tony: // \↗ But I wore a TIE //

Explanation: \↗ presenting this as sth. they both associate with interview clothing.

Lisa: ... // \↗ you SAID the right things // ...

Explanation: \↗ referring to what Tony told her earlier in the conversation.

3. (1) A (2) A (3) B (4) B

4. (1) A (2) B (3) A (4) A

Unit 17

【Section 1】

	name of the shop	the clues that help you decide
1	A bank	cash How would you like it? Could I have some fives and a few one pound coins, please?
2	A delicatessen or a cheese-shop or a supermarket	Cheddar.
3	The butchers	to have with biscuits. It's mature, and quite strong. I'd like some nice lamb chops, please.
4	A shoe shop	I like the style very much, and they're very comfortable. Yes, they fit extremely well. Could I try them on?

续表

5	The bakers	A large wholemeal loaf, please. And a half-a-dozen soft white rolls. They're for hamburgers.
6	Green grocers	I'd like some sprouts, Alf, please. I'll have some beans, then. Have you got any avocados? A lettuce and a cucumber, please.
7	A hardware shop	Have you got any of that stuff for getting stains out of furniture? Do you mean that sort that comes in bottles? Do you want large, small or medium? I need some nails, some six-inch nails.
8	newsagents	Twenty Benson and Hedges, please. King size? No, just the ordinary ones. Oh, and some matches please. Do you have any computer magazines? the middle shelf.

【Section 2】

Task 3

(1) J (2) E (3) B (4) F (5) I

(6) H (7) A (8) C (9) G (10) D

【Section 3】

Task 1

(1) D (2) C (3) D

【Section 4】

Task 2

1. the doctor 2. the bank manger

Unit 18

【Section 1】

Task

1

Check for breathing. Listen at the mouth and nose.

4

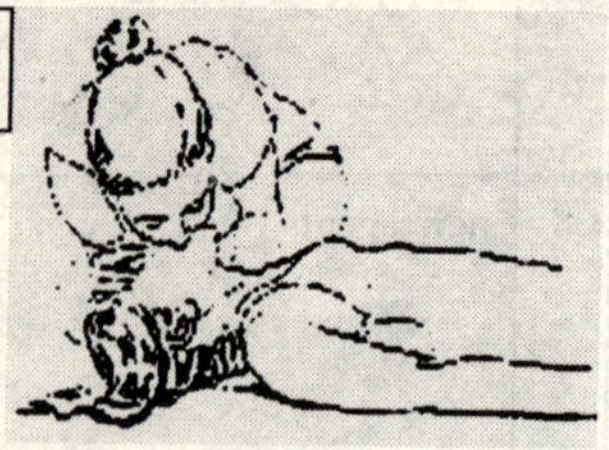

Make a tight seal over the mouth. Give the first four breaths as quickly as possible.

2

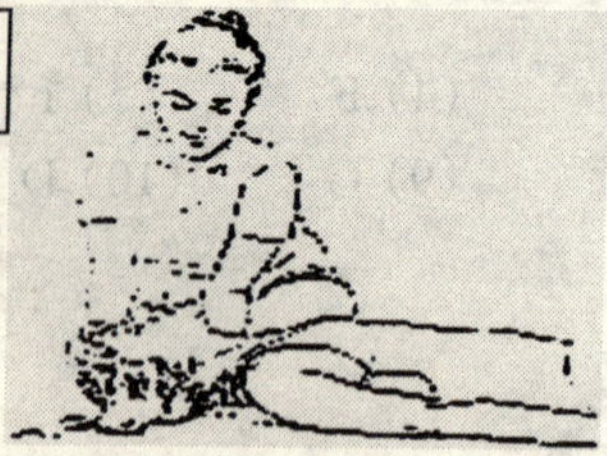

Lift the neck from behind and press down on the forehead.

3

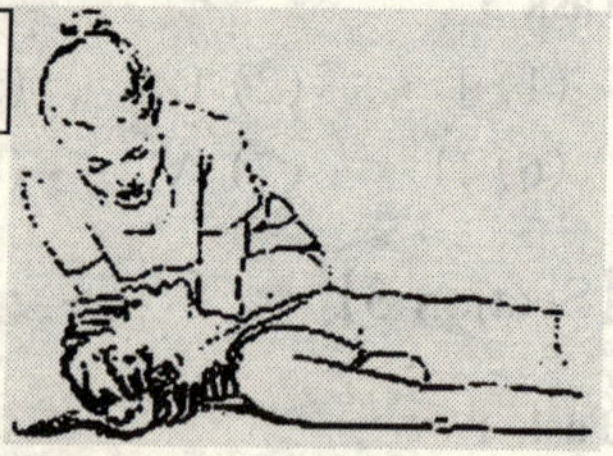

Pinch the nostrils and keep pressure on the forehead.

5 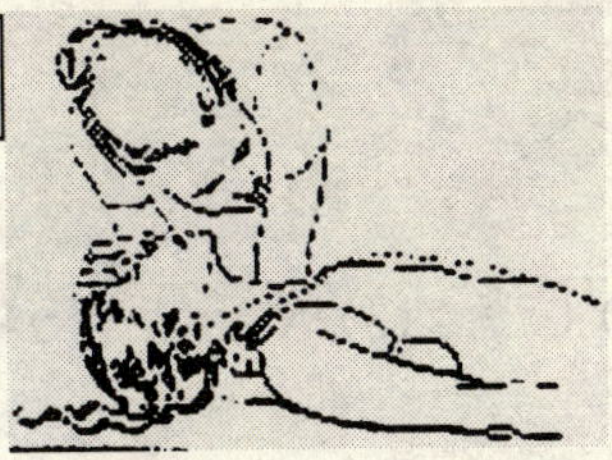

Breathe every <u>five</u> seconds and check if the <u>chest</u> is falling.

【Section 2】

Barbara	David
1. He's so inconsiderate. 2. When he gets home, he expects me to run around and get dinner on the table. He never does anything in the house. 3. He invited three of his friends to come over for a drink. He didn't tell me to expect them. 4. He's so messy. He's worse than the kids. I always have to remind him to pick up his clothes. He just throws them on the floor. After all, I'm not his maid. I have my own career.	1. I try to help. I always help her with the dishes, and I help Gary and Debbie to do their homework while she makes dinner. But she doesn't think that's enough. 2. And Barbar...she never allows me to suggest anything about the house or about the kids. We always have the same arguments. She has her own opinions and that's it. 3. She thinks they're too young to ride in the traffic. But I think they should. She always complains about picking them up at school. But they can't be tied to their mother's apron strings all their lives, can they?

【Section 3】

Task 1

(1) D (2) C (3) A

【Section 4】

Part 2

2. (1) $(2+3)\times 5=25$ (2) $2+(3\times 5)=17$

(3) $3\times(3+5)=24$ (4) $(3\times 3)+5=14$

(5) $(3-2)\times 6=6$ (6) $(4-2)\times 5=10$

(7) $4-(2\times 5)=-6$ (8) $(6\div 2)+5=15$

(9) $(16\div 4)\times 2=8$ (10) $16-(4\times 2)=8$

3. ① 93, 98, 20, 58 ② 19, 39, 184, 29, 09, 34

5. (1) A (2) B (3) B (4) A (5) A

6. Alison is leaving work / she's been sacked / Her husband / is very upset about it/ They're moving / to the south

Unit 19

【Section 1】

Memo	
Call about apt. in <u>Gazette</u>	
No. bedrooms:	2
Rent:	$425/month
Includes	No. The tenants have to pay their own utilities.
heat? electricity?	About $35-$40/month
What floor:	2nd
Elevator?	No.
Washers / dryers in bldg.?	Yes. A laundry room with 3 washers and dryers.
Near shopping?	Yes, just a ten-minute walk away from Highland Shopping Center and a couple of minutes by car.
Quiet bldg.?	Yes. Neighbors are considerate and no pets are allowed.
Address:	44 Turner Drive North side of Highland Boulevard
Who to see:	Mary Benevento
Time:	5:30
Other info: Wall-to-wall carpeting A kitchen, a living room (dining room) and a balcony Ring the bell for Apartment 31 Bring $50 for a deposit just in case	

【Section 2】

Task 1

Tracy: (1) (3) (6) (7) (9) (10)

George: (2) (4) (5) (8) (11) (12)

Task 2

(1) He doesn't understand. He thinks she should start bringing home some money.

(2) Her mom.

(3) She wanted to become a receptionist for a dentist or a doctor because she likes meeting people.

(4) Because he is about twenty years older than all the other interviewers and he'll retire in a few years.

(5) Thirty-five years.

(6) He needs to get out more and wants to be useful.

【Section 3】

(1) C (2) B (3) B

【Section 4】

Part 2

1. ↑ each language has special ways to mark thought groups / but in English / the chief marker / is intonation ↓

2. (1) No. (2) Yes. (3) No.

4. (1) No. (2) No. (3) Yes. (4) No. (5) No.

6. Dialogue

(T for Training Manager, I for Interviewer)

T: and of course we're in constant/touch with them by telephone ↓

I: Yes / ↑ tell me / er / some of the sorts of problems that you / er / get and that would call for a / visit from / THQ ↓

T: Er / well ↑ one of the problems would be / where we discover that something has gone wrong..."

There are five different topics.

7. (1) No. (2) No. (3) No. (4) Yes.

Unit 20

【Section 1】

FREETIME HOLIDAYS BOOKING FORM		
Holiday Reference Number S515	Departure Date January 18th	Number of Nights 14
PASSENGERS NAME		
□ Mr □ Mrs □ Ms √ □ Miss	Initials P.	Surname Jameson
DESTINATION/TOUR		
√ □ HOTEL	□ APARTMENT	□ VILLA
Name of the place:		

ACCOMMODATION	Standard room	Superior room	Deluxe room
Single			
Twin		√	
Triple			

MEAL PLAN	□ Room only	□ Room/breakfast	√ □ Half Board	□ Full Board
COST (Per person)	$ 1,077			

SUPPLEMENTS	Accommodation	Meals	Departure date	Other
	$ 50	$ 235	$ 33	
Total price	$ 2,790			

DEPOSIT	CREDIT CARDS
Enclosed please find deposit of ______	Card No ______ I wish to pay by credit card. Signature ______

【Section 2】

Task 2

(1) H (2) D (3) E (4) I (5) A
(6) F (7) G (8) J (9) C (10) B

【Section 3】

(1) B (2) A (3) A

【Section 4】

1. (1) Hearing is only the first step in listening process.
   (2) Interpret. Interpretation is a mental process. The receiver has to decide what to do with the message received.
   (3) Receive information, solve problems, share with others and persuade or dissuade.
   (4) intensive listening and casual listening
2. (1) become involved in the material by making written or mental notes.
   (2) predict or anticipate the speaker's fortune points.
   (3) speakers for any non verbal clues that will help you understand the speaker's points of view and emotional state
   (4) provide listener feed back either orally or through non verbal nods.
   (5) avoid yielding to your stereotypes, personal judgment and distractions.
3. (1) relaxation, for pleasure, recreation amusement
5. (1) a killing
   (2) in Middle east a Jordanian diplomat has been shot in Beirut